Delaware's Buried Past

A STORY OF ARCHAEOLOGICAL
ADVENTURE

By

C. A. WESLAGER

D1246590

RUTGERS UNIVERSITY PRESS

New Brunswick, New Jersey

OTHER BOOKS BY C. A. WESLAGER

Delaware's Forgotten Folk, 1943
Delaware's Forgotten River, 1947
The Nanticoke Indians, 1948
Brandywine Springs, 1949
*Indian Place-Names in Delaware
   (with A. R. Dunlap)*, 1950
Red Men on the Brandywine, 1953
The Richardsons of Delaware, 1957
*Dutch Explorers, Traders, and Settlers
   in the Delaware Valley (with A. R. Dunlap)*, 1961
The Garrett Snuff Fortune, 1965
The English on the Delaware: 1610-1682, 1967

This book is dedicated

to my mother

ALICE LOWE WESLAGER

Publisher's Note

This volume is a facsimile of the original edition of *Delaware's Buried Past* supplemented by two new illustrations, an index, and a 35-page Addendum. In it the author comments on the archaeological discoveries made in the Delaware Valley since 1944 which are important in interpreting prehistoric Indian life in both Delaware and New Jersey.

Readers unfamiliar with the technical terms used in the book will find a useful glossary in Chapter 9, "Relics from the Past."

Preface

THE sciences have lately come into vogue in the field of popular literature, a trend that had its origin in the early part of the present century. The writings of de Kruiff in medicine, Andrews in natural sciences, Shapley in astronomy, Hooton in anthropology, Harrington and Speck in ethnology, and others in chemistry, mathematics, physics, psychology, dietetics, and geology have awakened a popular interest in subjects previously treated only in scientific works and dissertations. In scholarly form they held little interest for the average reader because they were couched in terms beyond his understanding. But presented in non-technical language in magazines, newspapers, and attractive books, these stories took new and fascinating shape and gave the reader a pleasant change from purely imaginative literature. The details of how and why science came out from behind its cloistered esoterism is in itself a topic of no little interest and worthy of popular treatment.

There yet remains to be written a popular story of North American archaeology, one that will relate specifically to the work that has been projected by professional men and the hundreds of serious-minded amateurs quietly and inconspicuously laboring in almost every state in the union. Along the Atlantic coast, for example, the Eastern States Archaeological Federation, representing non-professional societies of Connecticut, Delaware, Georgia, Maryland, Maine, New Jersey, New York, North Carolina, Pennsylvania, Massachusetts, Rhode Island, Vermont, and Virginia, is doing outstanding work in studying the problems of the past in its region. Nevertheless, of all the sciences, archaeology is among the least familiar to Americans, who generally associate it with ancient problems of the Old World. Yet New World archaeology is dramatic, romantic, and adventurous, and seemingly would lend itself well to popular treatment. Let us hope that some day the job will be capably completed.

The present story is only a modest attempt to picture the work of the archaeologist in a small corner of America. I have chosen Delaware, not because its problems are outstanding or even unusual, but primarily because it is the state where I live and with which I am familiar. Any other state would do as well.

The professional archaeologist will look in vain for any notable scientific contribution on the pages that follow. This little book is essentially a compilation of individual adventures for readers who know little or nothing about archaeology in eastern America and is not intended as an analysis of cultures or a technical study. Apart from the reading enjoyment which one naturally hopes it will bring, perhaps the book may be considered of some historical value in Delaware because it presents for the first time a complete chronological account of all archaeological work within the borders of the state, a task that would be far more difficult in a larger state. And, since the historian of tomorrow will seek information about what we are doing today, the latter parts of the story deal in the present, with occasional reference to existing scenes and living people.

Although here and there license has been taken in description and dialogue, all of the material is factual and should hold up under critical scrutiny. In striving for accuracy in presenting the data, the assistance of a number of experts in their respective fields was solicited and is herewith acknowledged with appreciation. Dr. Horace Richards, of the Philadelphia Academy of Natural Sciences, previewed the chapters pertaining to Delaware Valley geology, a field in which his own published material places him among its leading authorities. Dr. Frank H. H. Roberts, Jr., of the United States Bureau of American Ethnology, read and criticized the chapters relating to the paleo-Indian, a subject in which he is one of the foremost American scholars. Dr. D. S. Davidson kindly read most of the manuscript and offered many suggestions from the point of view of the experienced anthropologist. Dr. Frank G. Speck also gave me the benefits of his comments and criticisms, for which I am grateful. Dr. Clark Wissler was of assistance in suggesting source material relating to early archaeologists in America. Nevertheless these men must not be held responsible for any errors, despite their good advice, which may have crept into the manuscript, and I absolve them of any responsibility for my shortcomings.

Among the Delaware people who were of assistance, Dr. Frank Morton Jones and Mrs. Jones, who was one of Dr. Leidy's students in the last century, were most helpful in supplying information. Charles Ottey, of Claymont, who was personally acquainted with Hilborne Cresson one of the early Delaware archaeologists, was a source of data that otherwise would not have been obtained. Miss Jean Wigglesworth was most coöperative in giving me facts and data I did not have about her father; Mrs. Anna Casey contributed her skill in typing the manuscript; and L. T. Alexander gave me the benefit of literary criticism.

My friends of the Archaeological Society of Delaware, many of whose names are cited in the story, also deserve special acknowledgment, and I also thank the Society for permitting me to borrow liberally from its publications. Above all, I am deeply indebted to Archibald Crozier for his advice and assistance, and for access to the source material in his fine library of Delaware-ana; and to John Swientochowski for many of the photographs which appear on the following pages.

C. A. W.

July 1, 1944
Wilmington, Delaware

Contents

Illustrations

1.

The Birth of a Land

NEXT to Rhode Island, Delaware is the smallest state in the Union, and perhaps that is the real reason why so many Americans know so little about it. We are a people who too often measure things in terms of their bigness. A state less than one hundred miles in length and containing only three counties is not deemed of great importance politically, economically, or socially. If it possessed a Grand Canyon, towering mountain peaks, or even a national park to lure tourists to its bosom, Delaware might blatantly announce its bid for the nation's attention. But neither nature nor the Federal Government has seen fit to endow it with such attractions. Its flat and somewhat monotonous landscape, farms, orchards, and tidal marshes do not captivate the sightseer, and its conservative inhabitants do not choose to sing its praises as they might.

Yet for three hundred years Delawareans have played a vital part in the development of the nation. As one of the thirteen original colonies, Delaware became the first state by being the first to adopt the Constitution. The other acts of its people, its folklore, traditions, and historical background, merit attention by all who delight in reading about America's beginnings. In 1638 the Swedes and Dutch settled permanently on its shores, then came the English, Scotch, and Irish settlers, the Negro, and in recent years the Germans, Italians, and Poles. From the early period of colonization through the Revolution and Civil War eras, Delaware has much to offer to one seeking the romance of the recorded past.

Although the native of Delaware is fully cognizant of the

1

state's rich historical lore, the problems of the present and his
ambitions for the future leave little time for serious study of the
past. But even those few who enjoy browsing in old chronicles
find that one phase of Delaware's background is conspicuously
absent in the pages of history. The written records take us back
to 1600 but no further. Yet it goes without saying that before
that time the majestic Delaware rolled down to meet the sea
just as it does today. Its tributaries—the Christina, Duck Creek,
Appoquinimink, St. Jones, Murderkill, Broadkill, Slaughter
Creek, Cedar Creek and other lesser known and quaintly named
streams—meandered through Delaware soil.

Shad and herring raced up the rivers by the millions in the
spring of the year to spawn, although now the contamination of
the streams has interfered with this annual cycle. The junco,
nuthatch, redwing blackbird, purple finch, blue jay, Carolina
wren, tufted titmouse, flicker, and other migratory birds win-
tered in Delaware during the past centuries as many of them still
do today. The native nesting birds—the turkey buzzard, bald
eagle, blue heron, wood duck, fish-hawk, and scores of others
fed and bred in the forests. In the native hardwood forests, the
virgin white oaks, bald cypress, cedar, spruce, and loblolly pine
grew tall, and the plants and wild flowers thrived more abundantly than now.

This was prehistoric Delaware, using a term in its literal meaning which is usually associated with events of greater antiquity.
The scene in Delaware in prehistoric times was quite different
from today. Man also lived in Delaware before 1600 and he, too,
was quite different in appearance and mode of life from modern
dwellers in the state. He could not read or write which is the
principal reason why nothing can be found pertaining to him
by those who seek knowledge in printed pages. Like the other
pre-literate aborigines who lived in America, he has been typed
with a careless, loose, meaningless term—Indian.

Why the term, which originated with Christopher Columbus
in 1492 was perpetuated in the vocabularies of the later explorers, who by then knew that they were not in India, defies
explanation. Nevertheless, they called every native they saw

anywhere in America an Indian. The Penobscot of Maine, the Mohegan of Connecticut, the Iroquois Confederacy of New York, the Powhatan tribes of Virginia, the Cherokee and Creek to the south and hundreds of other native groups were all considered to be of one breed. Among these were also included the "stone boilers" of Washington and Oregon; the powerful roving tribes of the great American plains; the sedentary Pueblo peoples of the Southwest, America's first apartment house builders whose descendants still till their ancestral fields; the civilized Aztecs of Central Mexico; the famous Mayas of Guatemala and Yucatan, the world's greatest astronomers until the modern age of science; the socialistic empire-building Incas of Peru; as well as such local peoples as the Lenni Lenape, Nanticoke, Choptank, Assateague, Pocomoke, Wiccomiss, Accomack, Accohannock, Ozinies and Tockwhogh of the Delmarva Peninsula—all were called Indians.

Now we realize how inappropriate this misnomer actually was, because these several native tribes spoke different languages and practised entirely different customs. It is quite impossible to picture a "typical Indian" because the people we know as Indians varied so widely in appearance and dress. The conventional image of the warlike Indian, living in a tepee, speaking pidgin English, wearing an ornate headdress of eagle feathers, his body wrapped in a swastika-imprinted blanket which he laid aside as he went into a whooping war dance around the campfire, may have depicted some prairie chieftains during pioneer days in the wild and wooly west. Needless to say, this description does not apply to the members of most other tribes, for they did not live in tepees, wear blankets on their bodies or feathers in their hair. It certainly is a false impression of the natives who lived in Delaware in pre-contact times.

Once contact had been established between the so-called American Indians (and we will use the term in this story for want of another that is as well understood) and the Europeans, the former began to adopt the customs, language and dress of the latter. During the years between 1700 and 1800 the brownskinned native who was then undergoing gradual acculturation

with European patterns became less and less like his primitive
ancestors who had no association with the white man. He
changed his dress; began to speak differently; and through in-
termarriage between whites and Indians, some of the children
of his tribe, who were promptly dubbed half-breeds, even lost
many of their native physical characters. Unfortunately, most of
the conceptions of the Indian and his forbears are drawn from
the semi-civilized native of this transitional period in American
history. During that era descriptions of Indian life were penned
by sundry untrained writers and at last the quondam pre-literate
folk were given literary identity, not by themselves, but by
their conquerors, who colored their accounts to suit their own
purpose. In other words, when we read of Indians in Delaware
histories we read of the white man's observations made after
1600, offered as an authentic description of the aboriginal culture. One would indeed be naïve to accept such accounts as accurately picturing the life of the prehistoric Indian, although by
inference they supposedly apply to the historic Indian as well
as his precursors.

What of the ancestors of the tawny people who dwelt in the
forests and paddled up and down the Delaware streams? Where
can we learn the truth about them if we cannot depend upon
our historical sources? The answer is that our knowledge of
them must come primarily through archaeological research. We
dig in the soil where they lived seeking their cultural and skeletal remains in an attempt to piece together the story of their
life as we might labor over a jig-saw puzzle. We unearth their
clay pottery vessels, shell ornaments and stone weapons and
utensils. Through archaeology we hope to learn the complete
story of whence they came, where they dwelt, how they lived,
how they died and in what manner they were buried. We are
able to trace in part the routes of their migrations and to compare their cultural remains with those of other prehistoric peoples who lived before them, or at the same time. Although there
are no temple ruins or crumbling palace walls in Delaware comparable to the antiquities of the Old World, the remains buried
in the soil, today invisible, can be exposed by spade and trowel

to reveal a growing story of ancient life. Archaeology, in short, is a method of research, and its followers are not interested in gathering together an assortment of stone relics and bones. The objects that are so earnestly sought are primarily of value as an aid in interpreting human experience of the past. The amassing of such evidence is a slow and tedious undertaking, but it is the only means that has been devised to obtain an insight into prehistory.

The historic period in Delaware—from 1600 down to the present—is less than 350 years in duration. This interval fades into insignificance when compared with the eons of unwritten history that lie behind us. As we reflect on the mysteries of the past, we must inevitably conclude that our civilization is only a brief interlude between the past and the future. The events that happened in the Delaware Valley before the dawn of written history serve to illustrate what was probably happening elsewhere in the eastern parts of the United States. The subject transcends the sphere of strictly local interest and touches on all Americans regardless of where they live.

How long man lived in Delaware before 1600, what route brought him here, and why he came are still controversial questions that archaeologists are trying to answer.

* * *

For an intelligent understanding of the prehistory of Delaware man, we must first know something about his home—the earth. Of what materials is it made? How did it come into existence and through what changes has it passed? This subject falls within the realm of the geologist rather than the archaeologist, but the two sciences are closely related in penetrating the earth's mysteries.

The earth was born, according to some modern geologists, about two billion years ago. Like its brother and sister planets, it was expelled from the womb of the sun and went flying off into space a white-hot glowing mass. Once it settled into an orbit of its own it became an insignificant fraction of the solar system which is only a minute part of the universe. As this molten body that was the earth cooled off it began to change its shape and surface contours. It expanded here and contracted there to form immense mountain ranges and depressions on its outer crusts. After millions of years of cooling the enveloping steamy vapor condensed and rain fell to fill the low places and form the great oceans and spacious lakes. In the meantime other natural forces were at work; weathering, erosion, decomposition, landslides, volcanic eruptions, and subterranean upheavals. In the last million years great bodies of snow and ice all contributed as they still do today, to alter the character of the earth's surface. It is through observation of all these agencies at work in various parts of the world that we can reconstruct their activities in bygone ages.

Today as we travel through the state of Delaware we see that most of it is covered with a gravelly deposit about twenty-five feet thick which was known to early geologists under the common name of Delaware Gravels, although the term is no longer used. Today it is called the Cape May formation of Pleistocene Age. The uppermost layer of this deposit is the humus in which we sow the seeds for our crops and plant our shrubbery and flower gardens. Beneath this fertile humus is another layer of soil which in part of New Castle County consists of a mass of red clay sometimes called the Philadelphia Brick Clay. Underneath the brick clay is red sand and gravel which comprises the remainder of the Cape May formation. In Kent County the brick clay formation is less dense and is replaced by a sandy loam, an excellent medium for sustaining the roots of fruit trees, one reason for the superlative quality of Delaware's peaches. Throughout Sussex County the brick clay formation is generally lacking, and the earth's covering is of a loamy composition ideal for agriculture.

This twenty-five-foot-thick stratum of sand, gravel, and clay was deposited in the time interval known to geologists as the Quaternary, or fourth great geological era which we are still in today; hence this stratum is Delaware's most recent soil formation.

Beneath the Quaternary and extending down into the very

bowels of the earth are many deposits of earlier ages, pressed one over the other and so deep they are beyond man's reach. They are composed of masses of gneiss, limestone, serpentine, and granite weighted by tons of sand and clay of many colors. In some of the sands and clays in the upper strata are the fossil remains of shells and other marine animals which prove that parts of the state were covered by the sea at various times during its geological history. The unfathomed depths of these subsurface strata have not yet been fully explored in Delaware, but geologists agree that long ago the state underwent successive periods of being submerged for millions of years and then arising from the sea as dry land when the water retreated.

The more recent layers, those of the Quaternary, have been more thoroughly studied, and scientists now have a good idea of how and when these later deposits came into being. Here lies a strange and wonderful story.

About one million years ago, gigantic bodies of snow and ice called glaciers began to flow down from the polar regions, covering the land, crushing the trees, and destroying much of the other plant life in their paths, and driving the animals into the warmer climate of the south. At least two different major glaciers visited the Delaware River valley. During the last inter-glacial interval, called the Sangamon, before the final glacier appeared, the sea level was about twenty-five feet higher than it is today, and most of southern Delaware was under sea water. At last the sea again retreated from the land, leaving behind the deposits of sand and gravel called the Cape May formation.

The last glacier, which geologists call the Wisconsin, spread over North America from the Atlantic Ocean in the east to an area between the Ohio and Missouri rivers in the west some time between twenty-five and fifty thousand years ago. It filled the river and lake beds, covered the highest mountain, and buried the prairies under inestimable tons of shimmering ice and snow. The marks of its icy fingers may be seen on the north-south striations on the cliffs and rounded tops of the tallest summits in the Adirondack and Catskill mountains, showing that it was several thousand feet in thickness. Slowly, relentlessly, this gigantic continent of ice flowed southward, moving under its own weight, but it stopped before it reached what is now the state of Delaware. Its southern slope, the perimeter of a mass of ice as high as a mountain, came to a stop a few miles north of Trenton, New Jersey. During this glacial epoch the Delaware River, carrying off the melting snow waters in the summer, was much higher and wider than it is today, probably covering an area ten or fifteen miles wide to a depth of three hundred feet. The land in Delaware was lower than it is now. Because of the proximity of the ice, especially in northern Delaware, the climate was too cold for human life to exist comfortably.

Finally, when the summer melting exceeded the amount of new ice formed in the winter, the glacier began to recede. The released icy waters rushed down to the sea, gorging the Delaware River with tremendous quantities of sand and gravel swept along in the current. This debris had been stripped from the northern land in the glacier's path as its frozen claws dug into the earth, and had been dragged along by the movement of the ice. Large boulders, which had not been crushed, were also rolled along by the advance of the glacier and were eventually swallowed up by the ice. As the glacier melted, huge jagged chunks broke away and floated down the river as icebergs, carrying the boulders with them. As the icebergs melted, the detritus from this glacial outwash settled on the ocean and river bottom, and some of it was spilled over the land. The boulders, relieved of their coats of ice, were deposited as we see them today, particularly in northern Delaware. Then the glacier receded to the far north, and the Delaware River began to narrow and assume its present size. Released from the weight of the ice cap, the land arose and took its present shape and contour.

More thousands of years passed, and the forbidding cold of the Ice Age gradually gave way to a climate similar to that of today in which man could live in comfort. Vegetation took root on the sandy peninsula, thriving in the sun's warmth, refreshed by rains. Springs gushed forth from the earth, and creeks and rivers sliced their courses along the land, making fertile valleys, ponds, and marshes. No humans trod the earth, but it was not an empty world. Trees grew tall and green until the land was covered with thick forests. Grapes, wild fruits, and berries of many kinds grew on all sides. Fish moved in the waters—birds nested in the trees—animals were born in the forests. Finally man came, first a dusky complexioned man who made his tools of stone, then white-skinned men from Europe and black-skinned men from Africa who soon peopled the entire continent.

Today, on the exposed surface of these glacial and inter-glacial deposits our busy civilization moves. Beneath our city streets, small towns, and cultivated fields, are the remains of the earlier man. Under his remains are those of extinct marine crea-tures that are remnants of the days long ago when southern Delaware was under the sea. When a deep excavation is made—the Delaware-Chesapeake Canal for instance—these ancient oysters, sea snails, squid, and other fossilized shells of univalves and mollusks are gutted out of the earth. But it is not these ani-mal remains, interesting though they are, that spur the archae-ologist to probe into the earth. He is captivated by the magic quest of learning more about human life in the past.

The tempting problems locked in the bosom of the little state of Delaware have drawn many archaeologists to the region, as the reader will presently see, and the tales of their adventures are replete with human interest.

2.

The Lewes Shell Heaps

THE story of Delaware archaeology began one morning in the
year 1865. A small party of tourists were aboard a steam yacht
off Lewes, a sleepy fishing village nestling in the elbow where
the Delaware River bends to form the Bay. The passengers were
mostly Philadelphians seeking the relaxation afforded by a visit
to Delaware's saltiest town, and an excursion on the water far
from the big city's noises. The names of these visitors, with one
exception, have long since been forgotten. The one passenger
in whom we are interested, Dr. Joseph Leidy, was a leading man
of science of his day. Dr. Leidy was the founder of American
Parasitology, a study that deals with the worms that infest pigs,
sheep, and other animals. His scientific interests, however, were
many. He was a professor of anatomy at the University of Pennsylvania Medical School, and a member of several learned societies where his knowledge of zoölogy, botany, and mineralogy
had established him as a scientist of versatility and erudition.

As the boat rode the choppy waves, Dr. Leidy rested his el-
bows on the rail and took inventory of the shoreline. His bulky
figure, long shaggy hair, and bushy black beard were almost as
rugged and picturesque as the landscape he viewed.

Leidy was not a historian, and he had little interest in the
historical aspects of the town on the low-lying shore. Here in
1631 the Dutch had built a little settlement called Swanendael
which was very shortly destroyed by the Indians. In 1663 Peter
Cornelis Plockhoy founded a community of Mennonites at
Lewes, the first appearance of the sect in America, but this community was also destined not to survive. By 1673, however, the

English had the area under control and a town called Deale had developed into a port for ships of trade in grain, meat, and timber. Early in William Penn's time the town's name was changed to Lewes, although it was more generally known as Lewestown. Penn ordered streets to be laid out, but the common land— the marsh between the beach and the creek and the pineland toward Cape Henlopen—was owned "in common" and guarded from private encroachment. Leidy's attention was directed to this stretch of common land, and from the point of view of the naturalist its scenic wonders were far more diverting to him than its historical origins.

Leidy saw the sand dunes along the shore looming up behind the common land and silhouetted against the sky. Seeming as solid as marble, the dunes, as he knew, covered a primeval pine forest. They were constantly yet imperceptibly shifting with the wind, grain by grain, through many centuries.

Leidy watched a buzzard circle above the dunes and finally dip down to the salt flats to gorge on carrion that lay hidden from sight in the cattails. Along the bank a pair of plovers were feeding on sand flies, avoiding the splash of the waves with short mincing steps.

As his eyes focused on these smaller objects along the shore with his characteristic reverence for nature, Leidy's attention was held by a dozen or more heaps sparkling in the sun. They were about half a mile inland and between the base of the largest sand dune and the shore. His first impression was that they were smaller dunes. Then they became more distinct, and he recognized that the iridescent reflections were caused by the sun playing on the seashells exposed on the crest of the mounds. He squinted his eyes and held his hand over his brows that he might enjoy a better view of the heaps.

Two of the passengers, following their distinguished member's example, also turned their eyes shoreward, and were shortly speculating about the heaps of shells, as it was then certain they were. One offered the thought that the shell piles were all that remained of a natural clam or oyster bank dissipated through the years by the wind and rain. The other said he felt sure that they were nothing but waste shells hauled there by oystermen. To these remarks Leidy smiled but said nothing. After a while, he turned to the captain of the boat, a native of Lewes.

"Well, Skipper," he asked, "what's your guess about it?" The captain, without turning from the wheel, sucked at his mustache. "Wall, Doc," he drawled, "our folks allus said that they was Injun heaps, but we don't pay them no attention." "My, my," said Leidy, using one of his characteristic expressions that meant that he was deeply interested.

When the boat returned to Lewes in the late afternoon, the passengers had lost interest in the strange shell heaps, and went their respective ways. Leidy looked at his watch and started after the others in the direction of the railroad station. Then, captivated by the lure of unanswered questions, he reversed his path, and set off with long strides across the salt flats in the direction of the old Cape Henlopen lighthouse. About a mile south of Lewes, he reached one of the heaps which he had seen from the boat. He estimated its height as about four feet, and the area it covered about fifty or sixty feet in diameter. Not having any tools, he probed into the heap with his walking stick. He found that it contained an accumulation of oyster and clam shells mingled with charcoal and ashes.

He burrowed deeper into the shells with his stick. Suddenly he stopped and picked up a fragment of what he recognized as clay pottery. It was the portion of the rim of a crude cooking vessel. He knew at a glance that it was not made by a white man, nor was it of any type of recent pottery known to him.

Spurred on by the discovery, he moved to the opposite side of the heap which he found partially covered with windswept sand. Brushing aside the sand, he exposed a similar heavy accumulation of aged clam and oyster shells. In a few minutes, he had probed out several fragments of pottery similar to the first sherd. With his stick he shortly unearthed another object, also of clay, but larger than the vessel fragments. At first he thought it was a piece of animal bone, but after brushing off the charcoal, he found to his amazement and delight that it was a perfect smoking pipe made of red clay. The pipe was about four inches long, with a conical bowl set at an obtuse angle to the stem. The exterior was crudely but beautifully ornamented with figures of triangles and encircling lines which had probably been imprinted on the pipe with a sharp bone tool before the clay had hardened. He knew that the pipe, like the pottery sherds, was of ancient manufacture and was a rare specimen of primitive handiwork.

Pressed for time, since the day was already coming to an end, Dr. Leidy hurried to an adjacent heap identical in appearance with the first. Again he set to work in the shells and shortly rooted out an arrowhead of brown, flinty stone which he recognized as jasper. The stone point was perfectly shaped and had originally been designed to be fastened to an arrow shaft. The scientist carefully put it in his pocket with the clay pipe and sherds.

Upon his return to Philadelphia, Dr. Leidy awaited until the next weekly meeting of the Academy of Natural Sciences, of which he was a leading member and officer, to make known his visit to the Lewes shell heaps, as he called them. As the University was the field of his daily labors, the Academy was his scientific home. Before the members, at a meeting on June 20, 1865, he exhibited the jasper arrowhead, the pipe and potsherds, and asked that the secretary make due note of the specimens in the society's minutes. Urged by some of the members for more details about the strange heaps, he asked that discussion be deferred until he had an opportunity to revisit them and explore further with suitable digging tools.

The opportunity came the following summer. Dr. Leidy made a second trip to Lewes in company with John Cassin, a noted ornithologist, Robert Frazier, and William M. Canby, a botanist of Wilmington who was later to become the first president of the Delaware Society for Natural History. The four men, equipped with shovels and trowels, spent several days in the vicinity of Cape Henlopen, digging at random in the scattered shell heaps at the base of the dunes. Some of the heaps proved to be shell accumulations at the stumps of trees or on small nat-

ural knolls and were only a few inches deep. Others contained
shells to a depth of several feet. All of the heaps contained charcoal, fragments of pottery, chips of jasper, and stone arrowheads
in addition to oyster shells. Several beads of rolled native copper
were found, which had been part of a necklace. Their most
thrilling discovery was the fragments of a human skull, jaw and
arm bones mingled with the shells in one of the larger heaps.
Dr. Leidy pronounced them the remains of Delaware's prehistoric man.

In Philadelphia at the October 23, 1866, meeting of the Academy of Natural Sciences Dr. Leidy discussed the results of the
summer trip and outlined briefly to the membership his theories
regarding the shell heaps. He had the gift of telling the story of
nature and her secrets delightfully and lucidly, and the members listened attentively. The heaps, he announced, were aboriginal kitchen middens, or refuse dumps, in his opinion. The
natives who camped near-by at some unknown period in the past
had discarded the refuse from their meals and clam bakes until
a heap of garbage was formed. In the course of time, sand was
blown on top of the heaps and eventually the garbage was completely hidden. Only at certain times were the heaps plainly
visible when the shifting winds uncovered the overlying mantle
of sand. The vegetable and animal wastes, originally a part of
the garbage piles, had long since decayed, but the shells which
withstood the elements had been preserved. The stone, clay, and
some of the bone materials which had somehow been mixed
with the refuse had also remained intact, protected from the
rain and sun by the covering of sand and shells. The human
bones, he stated, were unquestionably the remains of one of
the members of the tribe responsible for the heaps. Perhaps
when he died the ground was too hard to permit digging a grave
with crude tools; so the corpse was laid to rest in the convenient
pile of garbage and covered with shells where the wild animals
could not get at it.

Dr. Leidy never returned to Lewes to further his investigations in the shell heaps. The press of more important scientific
matters in his own field required all of the time at his disposal.

To his students at Swarthmore College, where he later lectured on the natural sciences, he frequently mentioned parenthetically that a wealth of aboriginal remains lay along the Delaware Coast awaiting the investigator. He had not added any important contributions to scientific knowledge through his incomplete digging, and many questions which now arise pertaining to his excavations will never be satisfactorily answered. Nevertheless, then and there, Leidy had made the initial steps in archaeological research in Delaware. Dr. Leidy died April 30, 1891. Although he was lauded for his many scientific accomplishments, including the discovery of the pork trichina, few of his contemporaries realized that he was the father of archaeology in the state of Delaware. The University of Pennsylvania Museum owns a few miscellaneous specimens excavated by Leidy, including one of the copper beads and uncatalogued human bones, but the remainder of the material has been scattered and its whereabouts is unknown.

Today one may well ask what prompted Joseph Leidy, an authority on animal parasites, to dabble in archaeology? Under whose influence did he develop a curiosity in learning about early man? To answer these questions we must take the reader back to the first recorded archaeological excavations in America. Field research in the problems on antiquity in this country was a reasonable and inevitable outgrowth of the questions aroused in the minds of scientific men by the earthen mounds in the Ohio and Mississippi valleys. These structures, some shaped like gigantic chocolate drops, others four-sided and flat on the top, and still others heaped up in imitation of snake, animal, and bird forms, had been known since the days of the first explorations. The Jesuit priests, Spanish explorers, French traders, and members of later colonial expeditions who penetrated the wilderness west of the Alleghenies often wrote of these perplexing structures of earth in their journals and letters. There was great speculation as to the origin, purpose, and age of these man-made mounds, as it was certain they were, numbering many hundreds, indeed thousands. Not, however, until the flames of the Revolutionary War had died out and new settlers began to push west-

ward did the mounds come into the limelight. Then, almost
everyone had his own explanation of how the mounds had been
created, and most of the theories were incorrect. In 1799, the
American Philosophical Society of Philadelphia sent out circu-
lars seeking reliable information about the mounds.

There were, of course, no archaeologists in the colonies for the
authorities to turn loose on the problem and settle the dispute.
Even on the European continent, where precedents were set in
the fields of science, it was not until about 1830 that scientific
archaeology was founded. In that year C. J. Thomsen, curator
of a Danish museum, gave the world the first archaeological
truths; namely, that when people live for a time at one location,
a deposit of refuse or debris accumulates in which are found
their tools and implements. If this deposit is not disturbed,
Thomsen stated, the oldest objects will be at the bottom and
the latest at the top. If the original occupants move away and
another community takes root, their debris with implements
buried in it will lie over those of the older people. Through his
observations of the levels of bronze and stone relics buried in
the soil, Thomsen concluded that the modern or iron age civilization in Europe had been preceded by a people living in what
he termed a "bronze age" who had supplanted an archaic people
living in a "stone age."

But Thomsen's work had not yet been heard of in 1812 when
an organization called the American Antiquarian Society was
formed at Worcester, Massachusetts, for the purpose of probing
into the general field of American antiquities. One of the first
projects launched by this organization was a survey of some of
the midwestern mounds with a view toward answering the questions that were puzzling everyone. Caleb Atwater, a lawyer and
resident of the town of Circleville, which lay in the heart of the
Ohio mound country, was provided with funds for the purpose
of pursuing what we would call archaeological research, although the term "archaeology" had not yet come into common
usage. He promptly started work, keeping detailed notes on his
findings. In 1820 the society published Atwater's account of his
work entitled *Description of the Antiquities Discovered in the*

State of Ohio and Other Western States. By virtue of this project, Atwater deserves the honor of being named the first systematic investigator in the field of American archaeology. He had embarked on an intelligent quest for data; he had evaluated the material he had discovered to the best of his ability; and finally he had written a report of his work—the three essential steps in modern scientific research. As we know today, his conclusions were faulty, mainly because of the absence of comparative data against which he could weigh his own findings. This was not through any fault of his own. Swept away by imagination, and in keeping with the illusory views of his contemporaries, he concluded that the peoples who had constructed the tumuli were "moundbuilders," an older, more mysterious people who were more advanced in their culture than the contemporary American Indian but were now extinct.

Between 1845 and 1847 another and more comprehensive study of the mound region was undertaken by two investigators whose work was to be cited for years to come by American historians. Dr. E. H. Davis, a physician living at Chillicothe, Ohio, and his associate, E. G. Squier, inaugurated an intensive survey and excavational project and arranged for the Smithsonian Institution to publish their findings under the title *Ancient Monuments of the Mississippi Valley.* Theirs was the first study of the geographical distribution of the mounds, and they also attempted to classify the mounds according to what they believed were their original uses. Squier and Davis maintained that some of the mounds had served as fortifications while others had been used as burial sepulchres, temple foundations, and as effigies for native ceremonial rites. In the burial mounds they uncovered many human skeletons and a large assortment of stone and copper artifacts, pottery vessels, pipes, and ornaments. They too pronounced the mounds the work of a pre-Indian people whom they identified as the mysterious "moundbuilders."

Coincident with the work of Squier and Davis, Henry Schoolcraft (1793–1864) began a study of the Indians of New York State, and 1847 his publication, *Notes on the Iroquis,* made its appearance. Although De Witt Clinton in 1817 had read a paper on the earthworks of New York before the Literary and Philosophical Society, Schoolcraft is largely responsible for stimulating scientific interest in the problems of New York which was to inspire a host of investigators to start work in the area. Lewis H. Morgan (1818–1881) a corporation lawyer, was also a leading figure in the early studies of the New York area. At first the interest was exclusively in finding traces of the moundbuilders, and in 1848 Squier went to New York to continue along the same lines of research he and Davis had initiated in Ohio. Unfortunately many of the sepulchral mounds had by that time already been looted by treasure seekers or destroyed by the plow.

In 1850, I. A. Lapham, a civil engineer, was engaged by the American Antiquarian Society to delve into the Indian mounds that had been reported throughout Wisconsin. His account, published by the Smithsonian Institution, entitled *The Antiquities of Wisconsin,* also played a part in capturing the imagination of the public and in helping to excite scientific opinion in American archaeology.

Although there were many other men whose names would of necessity be included when and if a complete history of American archaeology is written—no less a person than Thomas Jefferson tried his hand with the spade at Monticello—those mentioned were among the first methodical field workers. While their knowledge was limited and their techniques imperfect, nevertheless their work marked the dawn of an awareness in America's archaeological problems. But the most significant impetus to the study of anthropology in America, of which archaeology is a subdivision, came a few years later, which brings us into the time of Joseph Leidy. Three of Leidy's contemporaries were principally responsible for pioneering the work that was to follow and which is still in progress in America: Frederic Ward Putnam (1839–1915), John Wesley Powell (1834–1902), and Daniel Garrison Brinton (1837–1899).

Putnam, a naturalist who became an anthropologist, was a pupil of Louis Agassiz at Harvard and was greatly influenced by his teacher on the importance of collecting and studying concrete data to arrive at valid conclusions. In 1874 he was elected curator of the Peabody Museum of Archaeology and Ethnology at Cambridge, and became Harvard's first professor of anthropology. He was a dominant force in the Boston Society of Natural History which, like the Philadelphia Academy, was instrumental in molding opinions in the various sciences. He also organized the department of anthropology at one of America's leading institutions, the American Museum of Natural History in New York City. Putnam alone is largely responsible for the acceptance of anthropology as a standard university study and for the inception of American museums in archaeology and ethnology.

Powell, a geologist and philosopher who turned anthropologist, became the first director of the United States Bureau of Ethnology when in 1879 it was organized as a separate department of the Smithsonian Institution. As a disciple of anthropology in Washington, he preached a gospel that spread far and wide, and laid the groundwork for the field research in ethnology and archaeology that followed. During his time the Bureau published in 1889 a monograph by Cyrus Thomas called *The Problems of the Ohio Mounds* which blasted the older theories. Thomas maintained that the mounds were made by relatively recent Indians, a premise that has since been proved, thus solving one of the nation's oldest mysteries.

Lastly Brinton, a physician by education who became an anthropologist, was the first professor of ethnology and archaeology at the Philadelphia Academy of Natural Sciences, and professor of American linguistics and archaeology at the University of Pennsylvania, from which that institution's present department of anthropology stemmed. Not a field worker himself, Brinton was nevertheless a brilliant, analytical scholar and linguist whose teaching made a lasting impression on his students.

With the anthropological consciousness created by these men, Putnam, the organizer; Powell, the gatherer of information; Brinton, the academician, in three eastern cultural centers—Philadelphia, Boston, and Washington—it was inescapable that the veil was to be drawn aside to permit a view of the problems in eastern archaeology. It also followed that the East was to come into its own as an area as worthy of investigation as the midwest, despite the general absence of mounds. Younger students guided by such eminent teachers, left their classrooms and laboratories, their fingers itching for field work. The influence of these three leaders upon the archaeological problems of Delaware was first made manifest through Dr. Leidy, and through him to others. Leidy himself could not escape the magnetism of his illustrious colleague Brinton, and in his associations with the anthropologist at the University and at the Philadelphia Academy there was a mutual exchange of respect and admiration. So, although Leidy was, as we have mentioned, the father of archaeology in Delaware, Daniel G. Brinton was certainly its godfather.

3.

Rehoboth Encampment

REHOBOTH BEACH, which lies on Delaware Bay a few miles south of Lewes, is a vacation paradise not only for Delawareans, but for some who live outside the state's borders. Its cottages, hotels, and tourist houses provide accommodation for the increased population of the resort during the summer months. In the fall and winter the townsfolk settle back to a slow-moving existence to await the next season. The visitor to Rehoboth, as well as the native, is not generally aware that the land now covered with modern structures was once a summer resort for Delaware's stone-age men just as it similarly serves modern man.

Previous to 1872 there were no houses within four or five miles of Rehoboth Beach, which was a flat, wind-swept stretch of sand in front of a pine woods. Near the water a plank shed had been erected as a shelter by fishermen and bird hunters—the only evidence of human industry on the shoreline. Directly in the rear of what is now the beach, and not over five hundred feet away from the surf, were the remains of the aboriginal summer resort. It ran in a direct north-south line, paralleling the shore, protected from the tides by a sand bluff six feet high. The site of the encampment was level, and the sand was pounded down as hard as a macadamized road.

Skirting the western boundary was a freak of nature: three fresh-water ponds lying within a stone's throw of the salt water. The ponds were fed by hidden springs, and the water was cool and refreshing to drink. Scattered irregularly over the site were the remains of what seem to have been several hundred camp fires—small conical elevations composed of clay, oyster, and

21

mussel shells, and charcoal covered with sand. Some of these mounds retained their original form, while others had been obliterated by natural forces. Their former locations were evidenced by fragments of bleached shells and patches of charcoal and earth stained red by fire. The beating rains for years past had not changed this discoloration.

To this site in 1870 came an amateur archaeologist and collector of stone-age relics named Francis Jordan, a Philadelphian. A wanderer of the waterways of New Jersey, Delaware, and Maryland, he was a diligent student of the people who had occupied the coastal region in prehistoric times. Although his business was importing chemicals, he found time to pursue his archaeological hobby over week-ends and during summer vacation periods. Jordan knew of Dr. Leidy's previous visits to the Lewes shell heaps from the minutes of the Academy of Natural Sciences, and he was told by sportsmen friends that there were also stone relics to be found along the shore at Rehoboth. He was soon convinced that his visit was worth while, for the site was unlike anything he had seen before in his travels along the eastern seaboard. It was more extensive in area than any he had ever visited, and because it was then off the beaten path it had escaped the curio hunter. It was, in truth, an archaeologist's dream. Again and again, as the opportunity presented, Jordan revisited Rehoboth to spade into the remains of the campfires in search of relics of a bygone people. He uncovered many fragments of pottery that had been discarded centuries before, of the same type that Dr. Leidy had found near Lewes.

The largest of the sherds was no bigger than his hand, yet they were typical examples of primitive ceramic art. From careful study of these fragments he was able to reconstruct the process of pottery manufacture. The pre-literate potter had first obtained suitable clay with which he mixed powdered seashells. The shells served the purpose of tempering the clay so that the vessel would retain its shape and strength. The clay was then kneaded and rolled between the hands into long rope-like strands. These strands were next coiled spirally, one on the other, and the pot took shape. The sides were smoothed out to obliterate the coils. The exterior was gently paddled with a flat piece of wood wrapped with tough grasses. This gave the pot a surface rough to touch, but it left the clay more compact and durable. The marks of the grass-wrapped paddle were plainly visible on the sherds he excavated.

While the clay was still soft, the vessel was laid beside a hot fire to dry and harden through baking. The finished vessels were used for cooking and as water carriers or storage containers. From inspecting the fragments Jordan recognized that some of the vessels had round bottoms and slightly flared rims. Others, presumably so designed to permit them to stand upright in the fire supported by hearthstones, were egg-shaped at the bottom. Their sizes varied from small cups to vessels that would hold more than a gallon. The vessels had no handles and the surfaces were not glazed like modern pottery. Some of the fragments belonged to the same pot and he was able to cement them together, but it was impossible to make a complete restoration of a single vessel.

From the fireplace, and in the surrounding area, he unearthed many hammerstones. About the size of a tennis ball, the hammerstone had a slight depression on the top and another on the bottom to fit the thumb and index finger. That they had been used as hammers in the manufacture of stone tools and the refinement of potter's clay was evidenced by their battered surfaces. Large quantities of flint and jasper chips and unfinished arrowheads—rejectage of manufacture—were also found in the sand. He also troweled out scores of perfect arrowheads, mostly formed like equilateral triangles and without the characteristic stems of the more usual arrowhead. These triangular points might have been tied to arrowshafts with strips of leather or fastened with glue made from deer hoofs. He established the fact that deer and dogs were known to the inhabitants when he uncovered fragmentary bones of these animals in one of the fireplaces.

Primarily a collector of choice objects, Jordan was delighted one day when his spade turned up a perfect celt, or chisel made of stone. It had probably been used in canoe-making, much after the fashion that a chisel is used today. It was made of a black stone polished bright by having been rubbed with another stone, and the blade was surprisingly sharp where the abrading stone had rubbed a cutting edge. Another oddity he found was a paint pot or palette fashioned from a shell. In its interior a yellowish deposit was all that remained of the ochre once used as decorative face paint. His most noteworthy discovery was thirty copper beads, made of unwelded virgin copper, rolled into small cylinders from a quarter to half an inch in length, which had once adorned the neck of some proud native. The copper must have been brought from some distant point, probably the Lake Superior region, because deposits of this metal are unknown in Delaware. The beads were identical in type with those Dr. Leidy had excavated at Lewes, and none like them have been found since in the state.

Jordan was puzzled for a time over the exact purpose of the aboriginal site at Rehoboth. It was obvious that it dated before the coming of the white man, because there was no iron, glass, or other material mixed with native cultural remains that could be ascribed to colonial manufacture. He also believed that the location had not been a former native town or village. Despite careful search, he was unsuccessful in finding any traces of human burials, which are usually present on aboriginal village sites in the coastal area. Moreover, various artifacts characteristic of community life, such as stone agricultural tools, were absent. It was also apparent to him that while Rehoboth was ideally suited for summer residence, it was a less desirable location during the winter months than along one of the streams in the interior. The icy winds and snows that swept in from the bay in winter over the unprotected shore would have played havoc with a summer seaside community.

Finally he reached a conclusion which no one has yet had reason to challenge. He decided that the occupants of the encampment were not permanent settlers there. He believed they were residents of inland villages probably not far distant who came annually to the coast to escape the heat and to gather shellfish for winter use. The place was excellent for such a summer

fishing camp. The fresh-water ponds provided an unlimited supply of drinking water, an essential need in any community. The
waters of the bay teemed with oysters, clams, conches, crabs,
turtles, and fish of diverse species. Many ducks, geese, and other
edible wild fowl nested in the vicinity. The black duck, pintail,
teal, widgeon, and mallard lived in the marshes. The diving
ducks—canvasback, redhead, bluebill, and others now vanished,
lived on the ponds. The surrounding pine forest was well
stocked with deer, bear, rabbits, and other wild animals which
could be eaten and whose furs could be made into clothing.
The dried tree limbs furnished firewood, and the trunks could be
hollowed out into sturdy dugouts to navigate the bay waters.
The tree limbs could also be used in erecting crude huts or
lean-tos to shelter the campers, but these had, of course, fallen
apart and decayed. All that remained visible to the eye to mark
the encampment was the surface pounded hard by tramping
feet and the remains of the fireplaces. Here the natives boiled
and baked their fish and dried their oysters, probably in the
smoke of the campfires. When autumn came they trekked back
to their inland villages, carrying the dried oysters and clams with
them for winter use, leaving the shells and other camp waste
behind on the beach. Season after season they followed the same
cycle.

It was inevitable that a site which accommodated hundreds
of persons year after year should be marked with telltale evidences of the visitors. One is reminded that in the ruins of a deserted house there are always traces of the former occupants
in the fragments of glass, metal, and broken utensils. The broken
clay pottery excavated by Jordan represented refuse the Indian
occupants had left behind. The unbroken arrowheads had
doubtless been lost or mislaid, which also was unpreventable,
especially since the points had been chipped out on the site.
Wherever man lives, he leaves his traces in the soil—either in
broken domestic articles or lost or discarded implements, and
the ancient residents of Rehoboth were no exception.

With regret Francis Jordan saw the encampment slowly destroyed by the erection of modern dwellings as the resort de-

veloped. Hotels and cottages replaced the site of the aboriginal huts, and he lived to see the ancient camp entirely obliterated by the march of progress before he could complete his studies. With sincere but unavailing protest, he addressed the members of the Numismatic and Antiquarian Society of Philadelphia, of which he was a vice-president, in 1880, to lament the destruction of this rare site. Fortunately his remarks on that occasion have been preserved, and like the minutes recording Dr. Leidy's two trips to Lewes, are the earliest archaeological records of Delaware.

*   *   *

About 1879, Francis Jordan's attention was next turned to the area lying between Rehoboth Beach and the town of Lewes. Three miles north of Rehoboth lay a narrow strip of ground in a salt meadow then called Long Neck Branch. No habitation was visible except the top of Cape Henlopen Light looming up from the sand dunes. This lighthouse was built in 1784 (to succeed a lighthouse erected in 1767) after the British had destroyed it during the Revolution. In 1926 a heavy storm caused the lighthouse to topple over, and it has not been rebuilt. Within the memory of local informants who guided him to Long Neck the land had projected into an inlet to the sea. But the sea had since been held back by dikes, and Long Neck arose like a camel's hump in a salt meadow that could be safely crossed on foot. The hump of land, triangular in shape, was one-half mile long and about one-quarter mile wide at its base. Almost all of it had been covered by a shell deposit, as Jordan learned when he sank his shovel into several inches of humus that had gathered on top of the shells. The shells varied in depth from three to six feet and consisted of countless thousands of clams, oysters, and conches, all broken open for their contents. Beneath the shells was the original surface of the earth on which they had been strewn.

Unlike the scattered fireplaces at Rehoboth, or the shell heaps at Lewes, the entire neck was one vast shell deposit, obviously the redolent result of human industry. Mingled with the shells were potsherds, more numerous than at the Rehoboth encampment, and many animal bones. Most of the bones were yellowed with age, and had been split lengthwise. Jordan knew that this resulted from the native custom of eating every ounce of bone marrow, considered a rare delicacy. Here and there were self-contained areas heavily charged with charcoal and ashes that had been well preserved from the weather by the protective layer of humus.

The original peninsula had been an aboriginal fishing post near a rich oyster bed, between the larger encampments at Lewes and Rehoboth, Jordan concluded. Because of its temporary nature he did not expect to find any valuable relics, and his random excavations did not, indeed, yield any of the larger and finer class of stone tools and ornaments that he sought. He deduced that the shells represented the refuse of an aboriginal "oyster bake." Here a few native families gathered to camp and fish. They built fires to prepare their food and to keep warm during the cool evenings. Like modern picnickers, indifferent to the paper plates and waxed paper that fall in their wake, the campers devoured their oysters and allowed the shells to gather around them. After a few seasons of such feasts, the shells choked the camp grounds and they presumably moved their camp elsewhere.

Continuing in his search for productive sites, Jordan explored some of the shell heaps Dr. Leidy had visited several years before. He found the deposits even more extensive than Leidy had intimated. Beginning at Lewes, following the bed of a dried-up watercourse, he traced a continuous series of deposits extending all the way to Cape Henlopen, composed of thousands of tons of shells. Jordan was told by an old man that, fifty years before, the accumulations were from fifteen to twenty feet high and their dazzling whiteness made them conspicuous far out to sea. But most of them had been reduced by weathering, and many were hauled away for fertilizing purposes by Sussex farmers who were unaware that they were mutilating an unusual archaeological feature for the benefit of their crops.

None of the heaps produced any specimens commensurate

with the hours of back-breaking work Jordan spent with his shovel. For every arrowhead or piece of pottery he unearthed, he toiled for hours to remove hundreds of useless shells. Fortunately he was able to add a few fine items to his collection, such as another large chisel or celt, two cylindrical tubes of slate of unknown use, and a stone mortar which weighed thirty-six pounds, formerly used as a receptacle for grinding corn into meal. It had two shallow cavities, one on the top and the other on the bottom, so that either side could be used in conjunction with a pestle or muller. Another rare object was an arrowshaft smoother: a piece of granite about five inches square incised with three grooves converging to a point. In these grooves the arrowshaft was rubbed back and forth to make it straight and smooth.

Jordan was especially interested in establishing the age of the shell deposits, a point which he knew was of unusual significance in the study of Delaware man. He had not found any European objects in the soil, only crude native-made artifacts, which unquestionably dated the occupation as having been in existence before 1600. The extent and depth of the shell accumulations further convinced him that they had collected over a minimum of several centuries. Moreover, no living resident of Lewes could remember any Indians having gathered along the shores to fish, which further corroborated his theory that the shell wastes were more ancient than the Indians of the historical period. One important clue—and the only one he turned up in his digging in Delaware—was at the Long Neck site. Here he found a pine tree stump whose roots had grown down through the shell deposit. He was led to believe by this evidence that the tree had taken root after the shells had been deposited. The annual rings in the stump were plainly visible, and Jordan counted more than two hundred. If, as he surmised, the tree was more recent than the shell heap, then the heap had certainly been there before 1600. How many years before, he was unable to ascertain. He was still puzzling over the age of the Delaware sites in an effort to compute a prehistoric chronology when death halted his activities in 1911. Many of the specimens he had gathered were scattered, but a few of them were placed in the University of Pennsylvania Museum, where today they are available for study.

4.

Claymont Quest

IN THE search for knowledge of early man in eastern America, which began to capture scientific attention in the 1870's, after the publication of Squier and Davis' book, another Philadelphian came to Delaware with his spade and trowel. His name was Hilborne T. Cresson.* A resident of Germantown, Cresson's investigations were made in northern Delaware between Philadelphia and Wilmington which was within convenient commuting distance of his home. His wife's parents maintained a summer home near Claymont, where he often visited over weekends and during vacation periods. His work in Delaware won for him national recognition as an archaeologist and was a factor leading to his later appointment as a member of the research staff of the Peabody Museum in Cambridge, Massachusetts.

In 1864, on one of his first excursions to Delaware, Cresson and a friend named Surault were hiking through the fields bordering the river at Holly Oak Station on the Pennsylvania Railroad looking for stone relics that had often been plowed up by farmers. Their attention was drawn to two farm laborers digging a deep hole in the field. In answer to Cresson's question, the laborers said they were digging for peat to be used as fertilizer. Cresson was surprised to learn that a peat formation, the result of a fallen forest apparently centuries old, lay beneath the sod, and he and his friend paused for some time to watch the diggers.

* Cresson's surname was actually Jones, but he married the daughter of a man named Cresson who had no sons. Jones took the name Cresson so that the name would be perpetuated.

Cresson saw his friend stoop to pick up an object which one of the laborers had shoveled out of the hole with the peat. It was a large piece of seashell. Even with the dirt adhering to it, he recognized that the shell had been cut into a pendant and that a hole had been perforated in its upper edge. Presumably a throng had once been threaded through the hole, and the ornament worn on the neck of a primitive huntsman. The shell was covered with a patina, or film of age, indicating that it had lain in the earth for a long, long time.

Later, when the opportunity came to wash the shell, Cresson had another surprise. He found that it was incised—and the figure scratched on its weathered surface was the crude likeness of an animal. At first it looked like a buffalo, and then he realized that the creature had tusks. Then he came to a startling conclusion: the animal was a mammoth. His heart beat fast. The primitive artist who had made the drawing of the animal on the shell must have seen a mammoth face to face, Cresson reasoned. Yet he knew that no man had seen a living mammoth in thousands of years, for the beast had become extinct in the eastern part of America at least twenty or twenty-five thousand years before! Therefore, he concluded, the picture must have been incised on the shell by a member of an ancient race who lived in the Delaware Valley at a time when the mammoth plodded through a forest, of which all that remained was a peat formation under the sod. The peat—the shell—man; all were contemporary according to his deductions.

Cresson presently sent the shell pendant to Professor F. W. Putnam, then Curator of the Peabody Museum in Cambridge, along with a detailed report of where it was found. He had read of Putnam and knew that the scientist would welcome any data to prove that stone-age men had lived in the East in glacial times, a point that had not been established.

Dr. Putnam received the shell with enthusiasm and later, in an address before members of the Boston Society of Natural History, he dramatically produced the shell "with the rude figure unquestionably representing a mammoth" as the handiwork of an extinct race, older than the historic American Indian. The

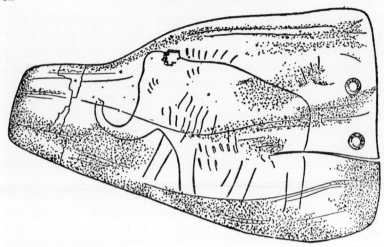

Drawing by Richard Stearns of the mammoth-incised shell found near Holly Oak, Delaware, by Hilborne T. Cresson and now in the possession of the Smithsonian Institution. The two holes were probably used to suspend the ornament on a string worn around the neck.

shell was examined by other leading scientists, and in 1891 was deposited in the Smithsonian Institution, where it is still on display, and has been the subject of debate ever since. Some persons, like Putnam and Cresson, believe it to be a truly ancient ornament and concrete proof of man's antiquity in eastern America. Others, more skeptical, pronounce it a work of more recent Indians, and not over five hundred or a thousand years old at most.

As far as Cresson was concerned, the shell ornament, despite the controversy it provoked, was his sesame of introduction to the scientific world. The same year a carving of a mammoth on ivory from a mammoth tusk was found in the cave of La Madeleine in France by Lartet. This spurred on the quest in America, and Cresson continued to give attention to the upper Delaware region in search of further clues of ancient man.* Several years

---

* In 1872 a farmer in Buckingham Township, Pa., plowed up half of a stone gorget, and nine years later found the other part. Known as the Lenape stone, it bore the incised likness of a mammoth being pursued by hunters. This object and Cresson's shell are to date the only artifacts found in the East bearing the likeness of an extinct animal.

elapsed without his finding anything of note. Then one day, while exploring along the shores of the Delaware River at the little town of Marcus Hook, he met a simple-minded old fisherman, native of the village. The fisherman showed him some arrowheads and spearheads made of a type of gray stone called argillite, which he had found. The specimens were badly weathered and to all appearances were extremely old. Cresson was immediately interested, for he had previously formed an opinion that this type of stone was used for making implements by the same ancient stone-age race who had made and incised the shell ornament.

The theory that paleolithic man had once roamed the Delaware Valley had already been advanced by Dr. Charles Abbott (1843–1919), a New Jersey physician and amateur archaeologist on whose homestead "The Beeches," south of Trenton, a large aboriginal site was located. Abbott based his theory on the reputed finding of crude weapons in the river gravels at greater depth in the earth than the remains of Indians. He theorized that there had been three stages of occupation in the Delaware Valley before the coming of the Europeans to the New World. Most recent were the Indians. Before them, and naturally with their implements buried deeper in the soil, was a race who made most of their artifacts of argillite. Predating these people who lived in an argillite culture was an earlier and much cruder people, still in a paleolithic horizon where man subsisted on hunting and fishing, and agriculture was unknown. They were thought to have lived at a time when the Wisconsin glacier was receding from the eastern part of the American continent or even before. All that remained of these earlier people were the crudely chipped stone blades, many of argillite, which Abbott called paleoliths and which he maintained were Delaware man's first attempts to make weapons of stone similar to the rude paleolithic tools that had been found in Europe. Abbott believed that the American paleoliths had been found in and beneath glacial deposits in New Jersey, but some scientists were unconvinced, and regarded his findings with doubt and suspicion. Others, like Cresson, were deeply sympathetic with the theory and convinced of its authenticity. In 1875 Putnam appointed Abbott a field assistant of the Peabody Museum, thus giving him a semi-professional status.

As we know today, Abbott, Putnam, Cresson, Ernest Volk, and others of the same school were ill advised in their loose use of the word "paleolith," which denotes specific characteristics and relationships of antiquity in the Old World. The term should not be used to designate a New World culture unless it qualifies in all respects, and of course their findings did not, nor have any subsequent discoveries.

Cresson, eager to confront the opponents of Abbott's theory with overwhelming affirmative evidence, was impressed by the argillite relics the Marcus Hook fisherman laid before him. In answer to Cresson's questions, the fisherman said that he had found the stone artifacts in the mud flats near the mouth of Naaman's Creek, a small tributary of the Delaware River which runs through the town of Claymont. He continued by saying that while cat-fishing in the reeds he had also often noticed the ends of logs protruding from the mud along the creek's edge like broken fence-posts.

Cresson picked up his ears at the new disclosure. "Did you find these stones near the logs?" he asked.

"Right alongside of them," the fisherman replied. "The tide must have washed them out of the bank."

"Did the logs seem old?" Cresson asked.

"As old as the hills and as rotten as punk."

"What are they used for," Cresson continued. "Who put them there?"

"Nobody uses them," the fisherman answered. "More'n likely the Indians in old times used to hitch their canoes to them when spearin' fish."

"Will you take me so I can look at them?" asked Cresson.

"Sure," was the reply, "but we'll have to go at low tide, 'cause they'll be covered up under four feet of water when the tide comes in."

Several days later, Cresson and the fisherman went down the Delaware in a skiff and rowed into the mouth of Naaman's Creek. He found the terrain on both sides of the creek flat and marshy and dotted with muskrat houses. Cattails and spatterdocks grew on all sides. They anchored the skiff at a little hummock from which the tide had receded a few hours before. There, protruding from the edge of the bank, as the fisherman had described, Cresson saw the ends of eight or ten log stakes. They had been driven into the bank by human hands, but their height had been reduced by time and only a few inches of each was visible above the mud. The mud had seemingly preserved the lower parts of the wood, but the tops had disintegrated from long exposure to the air. Cresson carefully removed one of the stakes with his spade. The stake was old, indeed, and it was necessary to dig around it, lifting out the surrounding mud in order to prevent the wood from crumbling. He examined the end of the stake that had been imbedded in the mud and found that it had been chopped to a point. But the cutting marks were not those of a steel blade, for the wood had the appearance of having been hacked with a dull tool.

The rising tide halted his examination and Cresson returned to Philadelphia, resolved to return at his earliest convenience to dig thoroughly in the mud surrounding the stakes where the fisherman had found the stone relics.

The press of other matters prevented his return to Naaman's Creek, and before he could plan other trips an opportunity came for him to go abroad and study. He embarked for Europe and enrolled as a student at the Ecole des Beaux Arts in Paris. He remained abroad for almost ten years. During his sojourn in Europe he visited many ancient ruins, including those of the prehistoric lake dwellings in Switzerland. The people who built and occupied the lake dwellings were members of an archaic race, historic forerunners of the modern Swiss and other Europeans. Originally their huts had been supported on log piles driven into the bottom of the lake, and the people dwelt over the water. At one of the Swiss museums, Cresson inspected specimens of the logs that had supported the houses and which archaeologists had excavated from the lake bed. He was amazed to find that they were almost identical in appearance with the logs he had seen in Naaman's Creek. He also noted that the logs of the Swiss dwellings had been pointed by stone axes, and it was plain as the nose on his face that the axe marks on the Swiss logs were strikingly similar to the scars on the logs in the mud bank where he had been escorted by the old Delaware fisherman. Here was something challenging to his imagination.

Following his return to America in 1880, Cresson lost no time in revisiting Naaman's Creek, and with the assistance of interested friends began to dig in the vicinity of the log posts. He found a number of stone flakes and scrapers—used anciently to scale fish—all made of argillite. In the creek bed he located more stakes, in a direct line from those in the bank. They were entirely covered by the waters of the creek, even at low tide, and only by probing the bottom with a long iron rod was he able to find them. He formed the opinion that these stakes, like the others, had once extended above the surface of the water, and that the creek had once been much wider than it was then. The bank in which the first stakes were imbedded had formerly been creek bottom, he believed.

Equipping himself with hip boots and a hand dredge, he began the tedious job of scooping out the creek bottom surrounding the stakes in the water. Bucket after bucket of black silt was removed from the creek and sifted. As he dredged deeper, he began to get bucketsful of peat, and with the peat every bucket contained stone-age relics—stone sinkers which had once been used to weigh down nets—arrowheads, spearheads, stone knives, hammerstones, splinters of bone, potsherds, stone axes, celts, and many chips of argillite, quartz, quartzite, flint, and jasper.

In November 1887, unable to contain himself any longer over a discovery which he felt was highly significant, Cresson wrote a letter to the editor of *American Antiquarian,* a popular scientific journal of the day published by the Society that had engaged Caleb Atwater more than fifty years before. He related how he had stumbled on the site through the assistance of the Marcus Hook fisherman, and had subsequently unearthed the log stakes and many stone relics. He inferred that he had found the location of former river dwellings of early man, similar in structure to the Swiss lake dwellings and of comparable antiquity. The log stakes, or piles, he intimated, were the supports of houses, and the stone weapons which had fallen into the creek bottom were made by the occupants who lived there before the dawn of history.

The letter was published in the magazine, and eastern scientists read it with amazement. Here was a revolutionary discovery which, if true, implied a mode of aboriginal existence unlike any attributable to the eastern Indian tribes. It was accepted as evidence in support of Abbott's and Putnam's theories of the existence of a pre-Indian man in the Delaware Valley. A number of leading men of science hurried to Claymont to inspect the log remains and the artifacts that Cresson had sifted from the muck. Among the most distinguished visitors were Professor G. F. Wright, a glacialist from the Bureau of Ethnology; Dr. Charles Rau and W. H. Holmes, anthropologists of the Smithsonian Institution; and Professor McGee of the United States Geological Survey.

Dr. Charles Abbott came one day on a visit from near-by Trenton to watch the archaeologist at work and to commend him for his efforts. By that time Cresson had also awakened the interest of some local men in his work, including among others, W. R. Thompson of Philadelphia, William Reilly, Charles Ottey, and Willie Shute of Claymont.

Cresson pointed out to his visitors that not only was the log structure an unusual one, but the underlying soil formation was likewise unique. Beneath the surface mud was a layer of peat—the remains of the ancient fallen forest. It was the same formation in which the incised shell pendant was found several years before. This peat layer extended under the creek bed, and some of the log stakes and stone relics were imbedded in it. Cresson sought to date the log stakes as contemporary with the peat formation, which would presumably have set its construction many thousands of years before when the trees of the forest were in full maturity. Unfortunately none of the geologists whom he consulted would hazard an estimate on the age of the peat. They willingly admitted, however, that the formation was due to a fallen prehistoric forest and was unquestionably older than the soil which covered it, in which Indian remains were generally found.

Cresson's reputation began to spread. When Professor Putnam, to whom he had sent the shell several years before, heard of the latest discovery made by the Philadelphian, an idea came to him. Why couldn't the project at Naaman's Creek, which was seemingly so important in the study of early man, be taken under the wing of Peabody Museum? He invited Cresson to join the staff of the Museum as a special investigator, continuing his excavations at Claymont. He suggested that Cresson exhibit his Delaware finds at the Museum and finally prepare a report on his excavations to be published by the Museum. Cresson accepted with pleasure, delighted at the honor of becoming affiliated with such an important institution. It was the fulfillment of an ambition that he had cherished for a long time.

In the summer of 1889 Cresson's work on the pile structure came to a premature end. The owners of Richmond's Brickyard up Naaman's Creek decided to deepen the channel to permit larger boats to navigate the stream. A steam dredge was used which destroyed the site of the logs, as well as the surrounding relic beds. The dredging, nevertheless, served to add new specimens to Cresson's collection and afforded him an opportunity to examine more thoroughly the geologic formation of the peat and soil. All of the specimens were shipped to Peabody Museum —more than six hundred in number—and Cresson later traveled to Cambridge, unpacked them and arranged an exhibit in the Museum. The collection also included specimens of the antiquated logs which he was able to preserve and which, with the stone relics, may still be seen at the Museum. Other specimens collected at Claymont were presented to Peabody Museum by A. B. Huey, W. R. Thompson, Willie Shute, and Charles Ottey, and as a result the Delaware collection began to grow. Even today Peabody Museum owns the largest collection of Delaware artifacts other than the local collections within the state.

In March 1892, Peabody Museum published Cresson's report covering the excavations made intermittently over a nineteen-year period on Naaman's Creek. In the published report he re-versed his original contention that the site was a village built over the waters of Naaman's Creek in ancient times. Doubtless discussion with some of his learned visitors provoked debate and raised questions he could not answer satisfactorily. After all, he had no definite proof that the logs were house-supports. He could not date the peat formation. He could not prove that the relics he found had not become imbedded in the peat as a result of floods or other natural causes. His main defense of the an-tiquity of the site lay in the specimens themselves, especially those made of weathered argillite.

He came to the conclusion that the log stakes were probably the remains of a fish weir, or trap, of indeterminate age. The stakes, he believed, formerly extended diagonally across the mouth of the creek like a fence. Withes of wicker or vines, he surmised, had been entwined through the posts, thus forming an obstruction through which the fish could not escape. As the fish came down the stream after spawning in the spring their exit was blocked by the fence. Aboriginal fishermen stood on a shelving or bank of clay to shoot at the fish with arrows or hurl spears at them. Possibly they also camped on the bank and many of their stone weapons and utensils were washed into the stream, which explained their presence in the creek bed. Fish weirs were recorded by early writers among the Indian tribes, and Cresson's theory at least had some foundation in history, and was entirely plausible if not conclusive.

Today science is still unable to explain the mystery of the pile structures in Naaman's Creek. Were they the supports of a water village as Cresson at first believed? Or were they, as he later concluded, the remains of an aboriginal fish weir? Were the stone relics contemporary with the peat? If so, how old was the peat? Nobody knows.

* * *

In 1889, three years prior to his published work relating to the pile structure in Naaman's Creek, Hilborne Cresson dis-closed to science through the medium of the *Proceedings* of the

Boston Society of Natural History, that he had made startling archaeological discoveries in Delaware. These discoveries, made in 1866 and 1867, proved beyond a shadow of doubt, he said, that an early pre-Indian man had his home in the Delaware Valley.

Cresson said that west of the town of Claymont, in the heart of a thick woods, he had encountered a huge boulder over eight feet high. The boulder was probably one of many deposited by the melting waters of the last glacier which may be seen today in the vicinity. It was only a stone's throw from a bubbling spring, and local tradition said that the boulder was a shelter under which the early Indians sought protection when camping overnight. Cresson, hungry for information, began to dig for human remains in the earth at the foot of the boulder.

According to his report, immediately beneath the leaf mold, he dug into an implement-bearing layer of earth containing stone tools, bone ornaments, pottery, and other Indian artifacts. He continued digging and beneath this first layer he found another stratum, also containing stone implements. Beneath these two upper layers, and at a depth of from eighteen to twenty feet, he claimed to have found fragments of a human skull and ribs, crude argillite implements, and paleolithic tools of argillite. The latter objects were imbedded in the red gravel and brick clay which, he maintained, had been deposited by the ice-laden floods that followed in the wake of the great glacier, many thousands of years before. Cresson's findings were accepted by some as further concrete proof of Abbott's theory that man had lived in the Delaware Valley at the time of the great glacier. The noted Professor Putnam agreed that the three layers, each containing different types of material, under the rock shelter seemed to illustrate the theory of three distinct periods of occupation in the Delaware Valley which Dr. Abbott had advanced. In the upper layers and nearest the surface were the remains of the historic Delaware Indians, beneath them in the yellow soil the remains of the argillite people, and at the very bottom, in the river gravels, the crude stone paleoliths of paleolithic man. Each, at different periods in the past, had visited the same rock

Rock-shelter site excavated by Hilborne T. Cresson near Claymont

From a rare photograph, 1866

Natives building a hut, one of several types of prehistoric dwellings. The two men in the foreground peel bark from a tree to shingle the exterior, while a third ties the cross-members to supporting posts with grass.

shelter and used it as an overnight camp. It was a rational theory, although Cresson alone had observed the artifacts in place and had no scientific witnesses to substantiate his claims. More than one thousand specimens were uncovered in the rock shelter and were sent to Peabody Museum and to the Smithsonian Institution. The most unusual objects among those now on display at Peabody Museum include a large neck ornament made from a clamshell and a pendant cut from animal bone. They are such unusual specimens that one who has never seen their equal in Delaware collections might well be inclined to question their authenticity.

Professor G. F. Wright, after studying the geological formations, offered the information that Cresson's artifacts represented an age of from thirty thousand to fifty thousand years, since he maintained the glacial deposit was approximately of that age. This was even older than the ten to fifteen thousand years of antiquity ascribed to Abbott's discoveries in New Jersey. Wright had not seen the artifacts in place before their removal but was basing his opinion solely on his interpretation of the geological structure which would be challenged by modern geologists. Not content with having eclipsed anything known on the American continent regarding man's antiquity, Cresson also revealed that he had made another startling discovery, a mile away from the rock shelter. On the afternoon of July 13, 1887, while following on foot a deep cut made by workmen excavating for the Baltimore & Ohio Railroad tracks, near Darley's Road crossing at Claymont, he saw a gray stone against the red gravel eight feet below the surface. He quickly descended the steep bank, and took out the stone with his pocket knife. Scarcely had be completed the operation when he missed being covered by tons of gravel which fell into the cut from the upper bank. Inspection of the stone object satisfied him that it was another one of the rare so-called paleoliths made of argillite, and he promptly reported his new find to Professor Putnam, who requested that Cresson continue to follow in the wake of the workmen digging a bed for the railroad tracks. Cresson did so, and on May 25, 1888, about one-eighth of a mile from the scene of the first discovery, he claimed to have found another implement four feet below the surface. The second, like the first, was also crudely made of argillite, and he immediately identified it as a paleolith. Both stones were later sent to the Smithsonian Institution and catalogued as rare American paleoliths.

Cresson's findings, however, were not unanimously accepted in scientific circles as bona fide. Many skeptics were not satisfied either as to the age of the geological formations or that the objects had been found in these formations. Since no one had been present to witness Cresson's findings, he was suspected of being an opportunist who was zealously trying to establish himself as an eminent scientist, by either fair means or foul. One of his chief critics was H. C. Mercer, Curator of the Museum of American and Prehistoric Archaeology at the University of Pennsylvania in Philadelphia. Mercer, a keen analytical student of prehistory, made several visits to Claymont and questioned many individuals about the rock shelter, the pile structures, and the shell incised with a mammoth. He learned that Cresson had a reputation of being a "lone wolf" in his archaeological work. Some said that the unusual relics had been planted—others said they existed only in Cresson's imagination. In weighing Cresson's discoveries in their relationship to the problem of ancient man, Mercer finally wrote that they "have been eliminated from the discussion by the writer on the strength of doubts current at Claymont and elsewhere on the accuracy of the observations." This was a polite way of calling Cresson a liar.

Although Cresson's work in Delaware was ended, he conducted several expeditions for Peabody Museum in the Midwest in search of further evidences of ancient man. Death abruptly called a halt to his research. After his death in 1894 his work was criticized, and he was not able to rise in his own defense and refute his critics, so the argument died because of the absence of a defendant. Later, as new discoveries were made, a controversy raged among eastern archaeologists on the question of ancient man in America. Was he or was he not a reality? The followers of the school of thought headed by Abbott tenaciously stuck to their guns that paleolithic man had lived in eastern

America. W. H. Holmes, Powell's successor at the United States Bureau of Ethnology, became the champion of a school of dissenters who denied that there was sufficient proof of a pre-Indian race, and refused to credit the evidence presented by their opponents. The subject finally resolved itself into a clash of personalities instead of a judicial study of data. Reputations were made and lost and close friendships were broken in the heat of the controversy. In the debates, Cresson's work in Delaware was almost forgotten and his writings were seldom cited. Today, in some circles, the subject is still argued. The majority of discriminating archaeologists, however, are agreed that all existing evidence indicates that the people known as Indians were the first humans to settle east of the Mississippi River, as we shall see in a later chapter. The so-called paleoliths made of argillite are recognized by the modern school as the products of Indian stone industry, undoubtedly quarry blanks intended for use in making conventional stone implements.

In the five-year period between April 1936 to March 1941, Dr. Abbott's famous farm was thoroughly excavated, under the sponsorship of the New Jersey State Museum and the New Jersey Archaeological Society. Professional archaeologists and geologists, including Dorothy Cross, Nathaniel Knowles, and Horace Richards, minutely examined every stage of the work and inspected every artifact before it was removed from the soil. Nothing was found to support the stubborn old gentleman's contention that a glacial or interglacial people had preceded the Indians in New Jersey.

The culture at the Abbott farm was pronounced to be homogenous and of no great antiquity, with no appreciable difference in the artifacts covered from the lowermost depth to the surface. Pottery was an integral part of the culture, and there was found no justification for an "argillite people" as a separate entity. The entire paleolithic myth was exploded.*

The work in New Jersey should seemingly lead us also to discount entirely Cresson's conclusions as applied to Delaware.

---

* Dorothy Cross, "The Effect of the Abbott Farm on Eastern Chronology," American Philosophical Society, *Proceedings*, Vol. 86, No. 2 (1943), pp. 315–19.

Yet an aura of mystery still surrounds the mammoth-incised shell, the strange pile structures in Naaman's Creek, the peat formations and the rock shelter with its allegedly successive layers of human occupation. These things have never been satisfactorily explained and they probably never will be. But they add much to the local color of Delaware archaeology and stimulate interest in the adventures into the past.

5.

Wigglesworth at Work

IN THE field of archaeology, the native of Delaware, true to his present reputation, remained unconcerned about his state until the Pennsylvanians—Leidy, Jordan, and Cresson—started to dig up his homeland and carry away valuable specimens. Then he began to open his eyes. Shortly before the turn of the century the hobby of collecting Indian relics, in which not a few men and boys then indulged, began to shape itself into a serious pursuit. Among the Indian hobbyists of the 1870's and 1880's, the best known were Fred Hilbiber, a Wilmington barber, and Johnny Jeffris, a legless enthusiast who traveled far and wide by goat cart, even to the extent of traversing farmer's fields. He was closer to the earth than his colleagues and could reach from his cart and pluck a specimen from the soil with nimble fingers. William Bayliss, Parke Mason, Evan Darlington, Charles Ottey, and Dr. John Cardeza of Claymont were also habitués of surface collecting. Among the hobbyists one became an outstanding collector and also won the distinction of ranking as the state's pioneer native-born archaeologist. His name was Joseph Wigglesworth.

Joe, as he was known to his friends, came by his interests, if not through heredity, certainly by environment. His grandfather, Joseph Wigglesworth, came from England after the Revolution and settled in Wilmington. One of his business ventures was a "Wax Museum" which he opened on Christmas Day 1834, at 15 East Second Street. There, to gaping audiences, who paid twenty-five cents admission, he exhibited wax figures, tropical birds, stuffed animals, freak fish, and other natural curiosities. One of his sons was lost at sea bringing back an assortment of strange birds from South America to be displayed at the museum. Another son, George, who also acquired the family penchant for gathering oddities, inherited a few of the old gentleman's specimens and kept them in his possession long after the museum was gone and forgotten. George was to become Joe's father.

When Joe was born on July 18, 1867, George Wigglesworth through his own efforts had amassed a potpourri of birds' eggs, nests, shells, odd-shaped stones, and a few Indian relics. Joe spent many Saturdays and Sundays with his father in the woods, and on one of these jaunts he found his first stone arrowhead. His fingers itched for more. As he grew into young manhood his interest in birds' eggs, butterflies, and animals waned, but he hungered to collect arrowheads, axes, celts, bannerstones, gorgets, and other stone relics made by the ancient Indians. Each spring found him in the tilled farmland around the edges of the city, searching for artifacts that the plow had turned up. He became acquainted with a score of sites of former Indian camps and villages where "when the field was right" he could pick up all types of stone-age tools from the surface of the ground. Thus as a "surface hunter" his collection expanded without the need of laboring with spade and trowel. From early morning until dusk, as the opportunity presented, he searched the plowed fields at Crane Hook, Edgemore, Hog Swamp, Stanton, farms near Churchman's Bridge, Red Lion Creek, and elsewhere in the rural county. Footsore and weary, he returned home at night, his clothing torn by briars and berry bushes and mud caked on his shoes, but his pockets crammed with specimens for his collection. He made many friends among New Castle County farmers who picked up the unusual stones they found in their fields and saved them for Joe's visits. He also started to correspond with collectors in other states and arranged to buy and exchange specimens.

Soon Joe realized that while surface hunting was an excellent method of adding specimens to his collection, it revealed little about the life of the people who had made the objects. He knew that the relics were the remains of a people who might be termed prehistoric. But the relics he found in the furrows were torn out of their original settings by plow and harrow, and he remained ignorant of the conditions beneath the soil. He did not know from what level in the soil the specimens were plowed, or if other implements could be found in deeper layers beyond the reach of the plow. There was no one to guide him in proper digging techniques and he didn't know how to proceed with excavation which he realized required knowledge and skill.

While on a visit to Ohio, an opportunity came to learn the approved methods of digging for ancient remains. The learned scientist Warren K. Moorehead, following the trail that had been blazed by Squier and Davis, was excavating at the time on some of the mysterious earth mounds in the Ohio Valley. One of the largest of the earthworks, known as Fort Ancient, was being studied by Moorehead's expedition. Joe Wigglesworth joined the crew of laborers in 1889. He found it hard work, and assisted in removing tons and tons of soil without finding a solitary specimen. But from time to time the work had its reward when the crew encountered graves of moundbuilders. There interred with the skeletons were such choice collector's items as copper breastplates, pearl beads, slate tobacco pipes, bone ornaments, and delicately cut spearheads and arrows made from distinctive chalcedony found in Ohio's Flint Ridge. When the crew found traces of such burials, usually first made evident by the darkened color of the soil, they stopped digging. Then Moorehead and one or two expert assistants set to work uncovering the remains with small trowels and brushes. Joe watched Moorehead with eyes that recorded every deft movement of the teacher's hands. He asked many questions. He learned how to lay bare an archaic pottery vessel, fragile to touch, without breaking it, how to remove the dirt from a skeleton and expose every bone without disturbing the position of the others, and how to interpret soil disturbances. Before the Fort Ancient project was completed, Joe was given superintendency of the job of opening Mount No. 65 and did an outstanding job. He spent many summer vacations digging in the Ohio mounds, not only with Moorehead but associated with Gerald Fowke and Clinton Cowen, leading anthropologists of the time. He learned the locations of other mounds which, throughout his lifetime, he revisited during his summer vacations for the express purpose of digging up relics to add to his collection.

When he died in 1937, Joe Wigglesworth owned the largest private collection of Indian artifacts in Delaware, and one of the most valuable ones in the East. An exhibit room on the second floor of his home in Wilmington housed the collection which represented the finest known examples of pre-Columbian arts and crafts. Some of the specimens were obtained by purchase; others had been given to him or were exchanged from other collectors, but thousands were the result of his own labor. In the room was a large fireplace studded with axes, pestles, and hammerstones, and many frames of arrowheads arranged in mosaics hung on the walls. One of the rarities in his collection was a series of tobacco pipes carved from slate and adorned with animal effigies which a steam shovel had gutted out of the earth in Accomac County, Virginia. He owned several dozen perfect clay pottery vessels taken from mounds in Ohio and Arkansas. He even had samples of maize cobs which had been preserved by the dry air of the basket makers' caves in the Southwest. He was fond of pointing out a small cedar chest to his visitors with the request that they lift it. It was heavy as an anchor and filled to the brim with stone arrowheads from Alabama.

Tiny birdpoints, shell beads, spearheads larger than a man's hand, stone plummets, highly polished bone tools, mysterious birdstones and boatstones he showed to visitors with true collector's pride. But the specimens of which he was fondest were those he had found in the fields within a few miles of his home. Primarily a collector who excavated for relics to increase the size of a personal collection, his motives are beyond censure, for the entire collection is now on public display at the University of Delaware. It was deposited there by his widow, who shared his wish that the collection should remain in the state. It stands as a monument to Joe Wigglesworth and to the extinct peoples whose handiwork was almost a religion with him.

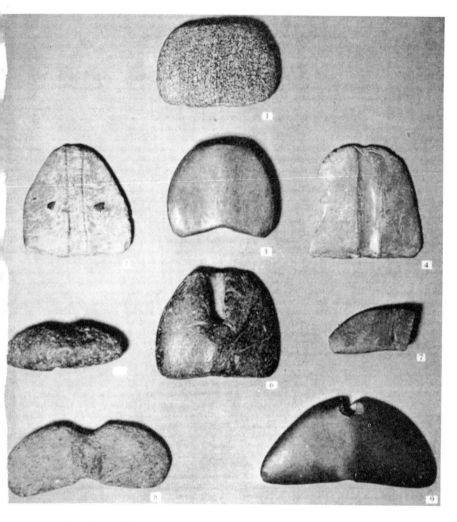

annerstones found in Delaware by Joseph Wigglesworth. Numbers 8 and 9 are typical
butterfly" bannerstones. Number 6 is a "tubular" form. Numbers 2 and 4 are not drilled
ut are grooved on each surface.

Stone gorgets and ornaments from Wigglesworth Collection. The black object in the lower center is a "sinew" stone.

One day after Joe Wigglesworth had proudly showed me his collection, I, a newcomer, asked him how he had managed to find so many Indian artifacts in the fields of Delaware when others who had resided as long as he in the state had never found a single specimen. His reply was indeed a valuable lesson in the methods of surface hunting and one that is useful to a hobbyist who wants to collect Indian relics but is ignorant of the methods to follow. "The reason I find relics," said Joe, in his gruff yet kindly way, "is because I look for them and know where and how to look." I, eager to learn his technique, pressed him for more details.

"To begin with," he said, "there's a big advantage in surface hunting. It's a good hobby that gives you plenty of outdoor exercise, and you can easily gather together a collection that will be a real source of pleasure as long as you live. No one can do any harm by surface hunting—I mean archaeological harm. If you give an amateur a shovel to dig for relics, he will certainly do damage. It will be unintentional damage, but he'll do it just the same. He will either destroy disturbances in the soil that are important to the trained archaeologist, or he will do such obvious damage as breaking pottery or ruining skeletal remains. With surface hunting it's a different story. The amateur gets a lot of pleasure, and he avoids doing any harm."

Joe Wigglesworth told me that the first and most important step in surface hunting is to find a site formerly occupied by Indians. He said that it is a waste of time to search at random for relics in fields where the Indians did not camp or have their huts. You might find an occasional arrowhead or two that had been dispatched at a wild animal centuries ago, but the hours spent in seeking one or two specimens can be more profitably used on a productive site. When you find a place where Indians lived, you are certain of finding implements and utensils they made and lost or discarded, he said.

"How do you go about locating an Indian site where you are certain to find specimens?" I asked him.

"The Indians who formerly lived in Delaware always made their homes and camps along the banks of a running stream," he said. "For some reason they liked to be near the water. They usually selected a sandy knoll where they would be protected from rains or high waters, and they often chose such a knoll at the junction of two streams. A location like this gave them the advantage of having their camps protected on two sides by water—like a moat around an ancient castle. Almost always there was a spring of fresh water near their camping place, because drinking water was indispensable in the life of the natives."

"In other words," I said, "if you find a sandy knoll along the high side of a running stream, near a spring, you might expect to find Indian relics there."

"Yes," he replied, "but it is not certain that you have definitely located a genuine site. You have only found the kind of location the Indians preferred—but not all such locations were necessarily places where they lived or camped. When you have assured yourself that the place you have found was occupied, then you can start to hunt. You can also be certain that there are other camps or villages nearby. Seldom do we find an isolated Indian site in Delaware. Where there is one, there are usually others along the same stream, within easy walking distance."

"Just a minute," I interrupted. "You've told me how to go about finding a site, but how can I be sure that Indians have actually lived there."

"Unless the earth has been turned up in some way, you will probably never know," he said. "You must remember that grass and leaf mold have gathered on the places where the Indians lived. In the centuries that have elapsed since the Indians left, the rains and flood waters may have deposited a foot or more of soil on the places where the Indians' huts stood. That's why it is so important to the surface hunter that the field be plowed. The plow blade cuts into the soil, turning over the dirt and bringing up the Indian relics to the top so they can be seen."

"You mean to say that when I have found a likely site, all I need do is follow the farmer when he plows or harrows the field?"

"If you did you wouldn't find anything at all," he answered

with a smile. "Newly plowed or harrowed ground is very dry. The dirt sticks to all the stones, and you can't distinguish a relic from an ordinary stone or clod. Everything is the same color as the soil."

"What do I do then?"

"You must wait until after a heavy rain. The beat of the rain washes the dirt off the stones, and you can easily distinguish good specimens from ordinary stones. An all-day downpour on plowed ground gives the field an altogether different appearance than when it was first plowed."

"I have heard it said that corn fields are good places to look for Indian relics," I said. "Is that true?"

"Yes indeed," he replied with a smile, "providing, of course, that the corn is planted on a former Indian site. When the cornfield is plowed, the plow is set to dig deeper in the ground than for some other crops. That naturally exposes Indian material that lies deeper in the soil. But, even more important, the farmer continues to cultivate a corn field until the corn stalks are almost mature. That keeps the ground turned over continually, which gives you a better chance of finding something worth while. Another thing to remember is that corn is planted in rows and does not grow over the entire field as do wheat and oats. Thus you can return to the field all through the season and hunt in it without trampling down the crop. Finally, when the corn is out, the field can be searched again. The beat of rains throughout the summer usually exposes specimens that you missed on your earlier visits."

"Needless to say," he continued, "you must be familiar with the appearance of Indian specimens. Otherwise you wouldn't know one stone from another. The best way to familiarize yourself with Indian tools and weapons is to visit a museum first.

"If you keep in touch with the farmers, you will learn when they plan to plow for corn, wheat, oats, and other crops. Then, by keeping an eye on the weather, you will know the best time to visit your site. Then all you need to do is to follow the path that the plow has made, taking row by row. I always carry a cane with a pointed end, which saves a lot of stooping. It's also a good idea to take several paper bags with you. You can mark on the outside of each bag the name of the farm where you found the specimens, and the bag is a handy container to bring home your stones.

"When you arrive home, always wash the specimens you have found and label them with India ink. I label my relics by the county where they were found, but it is better to mark them according to the name of the farm where they were found. Some collectors label each specimen and keep a catalogue where each is entered by number. That is a very good plan, because an archaeological collection is more valuable if you know exactly where each specimen was found."

"One thing more," I said, "you mention Indian camp sites and village sites. How do you tell the difference?"

"It's sometimes difficult to distinguish between them," he said. "Generally speaking, a camp site is a small site used as an overnight stopping place by hunting and fishing parties. You don't expect to find any large variety of materials on a camp site, except hunting implements made of stone. A village site covers a large area, and usually you find large quantities of stone chips, arrowheads, potsherds, and other remains of domestic life. An abundance of pottery is a good criterion of family life."

To those who would like to make a hobby of finding Indian relics, I know of no better advice than Joe Wigglesworth gave me. I might add further that I know of no hobby which is more diverting and at the same time satisfies the acquisitive instinct that most of us seem to have. His word of caution regarding digging should be repeated: unless you have had archaeological training, don't dig, but confine your efforts to surface hunting.

*   *   *

Few records exist of Joe Wigglesworth's excavations in Delaware after he had learned digging techniques from Moorehead, Fowke, and Cowen. Following his marriage in 1915 he busied himself in city and county political affairs, serving in both elective and appointive offices. The press of business and home obligations to his wife and children occupied much of his time.

Nevertheless he managed on an occasional Saturday or Sunday to dig at Crane Hook and on Briar Hill near Newport, although he did not make any important discoveries. The excavation with which his name is generally associated was made near Rehoboth Beach. It was not unusual that this veteran collector should eventually turn to Delaware's most prolific area which had been visited years before by Dr. Leidy and Francis Jordan.

While reconnoitering south of Rehoboth, Wigglesworth came upon a succession of hills and sand dunes along the coast between the resort and the Rehoboth Bay. By digging test holes he was satisfied that the complexion of the coast here, as between Lewes and Rehoboth, was freckled with the same type of shell heaps noted by earlier investigators. In fact, we now know that these shell deposits extend the full length of the Delaware Peninsula on both the Delaware Bay and Chesapeake Bay sides. He spaded into some of these shell accumulations, uncovering a few arrowheads, fragmentary potsherds, charcoal, and animal bones. On one occasion he brought out on his shovel the largest stone celt he had ever seen. But such unusual specimens were few and the results did not justify the effort, so he gave up. Joe was not a man to dig for nothing. Yet he was convinced that more important remains were hidden under the sand in the same vicinity of the shell heaps, but the area was so vast that he was at a loss where to dig. Then Fate guided his hands.

One day, after a hurricane had ravaged the coast, Joe learned that human bones had been washed out of the sand. He hurried to investigate. He found himself on a sandy bluff eighteen or twenty feet above the level of the ocean and not far from the shell heaps in which he had been digging. A few scattered bones lay on the beach below, still wet with rain, and yellowed by age. He examined the bones carefully. There was no doubt about it, they were human bones that had washed out of the bluff and fallen to the beach below.

Returning to the bluff he began to excavate, applying one of the trenching techniques Moorehead had used in digging the Ohio mounds. He spaded a trench three feet deep, four feet wide and twelve feet long, paralleling the bluff but several feet back from the edge. From this large trench he opened narrow trenches to the west and southwest, stopping from time to time to scrutinize the walls of the trench to determine if there had been an earlier disturbance of the earth. He knew that, once the earth had been disturbed by grave digging, no matter how many centuries might pass, the tell-tale markings in the soil can be detected by the practised eye. It is as apparent to the archaeologist as a white chalk mark on a blackboard.

Having had no success, he began to spade out the area between the large trench and the bluff. After his third spadeful of sand, he saw the black streaks running through the soil that meant an earlier disturbance, and the next spadeful brought out a part of a human shoulder blade. He immediately laid aside his spade and went down on hands and knees with his trowel.

For hours he worked patiently, troweling away the sand and the dirt and brushing the bones clean as they were encountered. He was careful not to move the bones from their original positions. He knew that only by observing the skeleton in the posture in which it had been buried was it possible to interpret its meaning. But, to his surprise, this burial was unlike any that he had excavated in the Midwest. The skeletons he had unearthed in the Ohio mounds had been buried on their backs or on their sides with knees drawn up, and the excavator could expose the skeleton as a complete articulated unit. As he looked down at what he had uncovered, he could scarcely believe his eyes. Instead of a single skeleton, he had found a group burial and the bones were all mixed together. Skulls of children and adults were mingled with toe and finger bones; leg bones were crossed over ribs; arm bones jumbled up with pelvic bones; and vertebrae were scattered among clavicles. Yet he was certain from the appearance of the soil that no one had dug into the grave since the time of interment centuries before. The bones obviously must have been cut apart before being interred.

In all, he counted the disjointed bones of fourteen skeletons. They had been placed in one large grave nine feet long, six feet wide and three feet deep. After taking all the measurements he thought necessary, and still puzzling over the strange situation, he sifted the soil from the grave through a fine-meshed screen. All he found were four small arrowheads and a few unimportant potsherds. Nothing of value to the collector had been buried with the dead Indians. He later reburied the bones, disappointed at having found no rare artifacts to add to his collection.

Joe Wigglesworth wrote a brief report of his excavation in which he concluded that he must have uncovered the grave of a band of Indians who had been massacred and beheaded by their enemies. It was a logical supposition in the face of the evidence, but an incorrect one. In the light of later discoveries, it seems clear today that he had actually but unknowingly excavated the type of ancient grave known as an ossuary.

The ossuary burial was characteristic of some of the tribes of Virginia, Maryland, and the Carolinas, and was also practised by several southern Delaware tribes. The Nanticoke, Choptank, and Assateague peoples, for example, are known to have followed a custom involving ossuary burial which seems horrifying to us today. We are told by early writers that the skin of the dead person was slit up the back and removed. The dead one's bones were next scraped free of flesh by priest-officials, using stone tools or their finger nails. The bones and flesh were then wrapped in animal skins and placed temporarily on shelves built in a log structure called a Chiacason House. Periodically the remains were collected from the Chiacason Houses and reburied in a large common grave, or ossuary. A ceremony was held in conjunction with the rites, probably with singing and dancing, and dirt was then thrown in the pit to cover all the remains. Archaeologists have note of a number of ossuary burials from the Delmarva Peninsula, and it is to be expected that others will come to attention in the future.

In the *Delaware Gazette* for 1838 it was reported that, thirty years before, a crew of workmen digging earth from a bank near a small stream within a mile of Laurel, had encountered a large grave by accident. Several wagonloads of human bones were removed, but unfortunately this happened in the days before the Delaware archaeologist came on the scene, and no data were taken. Valuable information was lost forever to science, but from the account one deduces that the grave was actually an ossuary.

In 1938 a state highway crew inadvertently stumbled into another ossuary east of Felton, Delaware, near Killen's Mill Pond. In the course of removing sand from a hillock for use on the highway, the separated bones of a dozen or more individuals were found. Many stone ornaments and implements, which had been laid with the corpses, were also removed by the workers. The graves were looted and the bones mutilated before the arrival of persons sufficiently experienced to uncover the remains in a scientific manner, and state officials have since instructed their working crews to cease operations when they encounter human bones or Indian materials in the soil.

When foundations for a jail at Cambridge, Maryland, on the Eastern Shore were being laid in 1833, an ossuary containing sixteen skeletons was found. Another ossuary was reported by H. C. Mercer in 1897, at Sandy Point where the Choptank River meets Chesapeake Bay. It contained the bones of more than one hundred skeletons, all buried in one large pit. In later years another ossuary was found near-by by workers laying the foundation for a sea wall. No one can be certain how many bodies had been interred, but many priceless artifacts—beautiful slate tobacco pipes, ornaments, and stone tubes—were dug out with the bones and carried away by the workmen. Once more, important data were sacrificed from selfish motives.

Today we are mystified at this burial custom, which indeed seems unconventional and disrespectful of the dead when compared to our own mortuary practices. Nevertheless it is wrong for us to pass judgment with our little understanding of the reasons which prompted the custom. No doubt it was the result of deep religious convictions, for the Indians considered their dead with greater reverence than we. We know that the Nanticoke Indians carried away the bones of their honored dead when they moved away from the Delmarva Peninsula, beginning in 1745, and reburied them at their new homes in Pennsylvania. These Indians, if they could come back to life, would criticize us for the perfunctory manner in which we bury our loved ones and do not cherish their remains once they leave us.

A few remnant Choptank Indians who lived àt Locust Neck on the Choptank River preserved the bones of their former chief, Wynicaco, in a log Chiacason House for eighty years. As late as the year 1794 the bones were still in their possession and were considered a sacred care.

The strange custom of bone-scraping, preservation of corpses, and reburial in an ossuary intrigues us and invites the archaeologist to dig deeper in search of an explanation. Somewhere in Delaware soil the answer may lie buried. If we knew exactly where ossuaries could be found it would be relatively easier to seek answers to our questions. Unfortunately the Indian ossuaries were not marked by stones or other monuments as are modern graves and, as we have seen, are usually encountered by accident.

6.

Slaughter Creek Search

IN 1933 news reached the Department of Anthropology at the University of Pennsylvania of the existence of a large aboriginal site about ten miles south of Milford in Sussex County, Delaware. It lay along the shore of Slaughter Creek in Prime Hook Neck on a large farm owned by Robert Jones, the site extending over the lines of the Jones farm to adjacent properties on either side. Many stone artifacts, potsherds, animal bones, and great quantities of shells had lately been uprooted by the plow during the spring planting. The news came at a fortuitous time, for Dr. D. S. Davidson, a member of the Department of Anthropology which Dr. Brinton founded, had recently inaugurated a project among his graduate students embracing the archaeological problems of the entire Delmarva Peninsula. At the earliest opportunity, the anthropologist visited what was to become known as the Slaughter Creek Site.

The origin of the name of the creek, which probably arouses questions in the reader's mind, is not definitely known. Slaughter is an old English name, and the creek may have been so called after one of the members of the family who settled in Delaware. A local tradition, however, says that an actual slaughter occurred along its banks. In the early days the Indians planned secretly to massacre the white settlers, so the story goes. One of the prominent white settlers borrowed a cannon from a vessel stranded on the beach and summoned all the Indians to meet with him for an important conference. He explained that the Great Spirit was about to speak to them in a loud voice and punish their bad chiefs. He then lined up the conspirators in front of the cannon, which promptly spoke as he had promised, killing the agitators and guaranteeing the peace.

After careful reconnaissance at Slaughter Creek, Davidson reasoned that an excavation would probably not only uncover valuable specimens and data but would also be a proving ground where his students might learn excavational techniques. He requested financial help from the University and a small sum was granted by a research fund to enable him to carry on the work. He also received permission from the owner of the property to dig in the fields after the crops had been harvested. During 1933 and 1934, usually over week-ends, Davidson and his students motored to the Jones farm to excavate in the fields. Dr. J. Alden Mason, authority on Central American archaeology and Curator of the American section of the University of Pennsylvania Museum, also accompanied the party on several trips. The student excavators included among others Loren C. Eiseley, now Associate Professor of Anthropology at the University of Kansas, Richard Faust, Louis Korn, and Dr. H. Y. Feng, at present an anthropologist in the employ of the Chinese Government.

In Delaware, by this time, archaeology as a science was at last beginning to be seriously considered. In March of 1933, through the efforts of H. Geiger Omwake, a Dover school teacher and collector of Indian artifacts, an organization was formed called the Archaeological Society of Delaware. Its membership at first consisted of approximately twenty amateurs interested in obtaining information and specimens relating to the early occupants of the state. Most of them, like the founder of the Society, were collectors of arrowheads and other prehistoric Indian artifacts. Davidson's investigations came at a time when the Society was in its infancy and in need of professional guidance in archaeological techniques. Therefore the members were greatly pleased when the anthropologist attended one of their first meetings at Dover and invited them to assist in his diggings at Slaughter Creek.

Once the work had got under way, the investigators were impressed to find that the site covered an area of perhaps one hundred acres, and they surmised that several centuries ago it had been an important aboriginal town. There were no documentary records in existence to prove this contention inasmuch as the native occupants had apparently deserted their village prior to the coming of the white man. Their enemies may have driven them away. They may have fled in fear when they learned that the whites had landed in Delaware Bay. Or, as so often happened among the coastal Indians, they may for economic reasons have moved their huts to a new village location.

Whether they were of a tribe affiliated with the Nanticoke, Delaware, or an unnamed Indian group could not, of course, be established in the absence of written records pertaining to their village and customs. The last and only available means of obtaining information was through archaeological research. The most conspicuous surface indication of the former occupation were the great quantities of bleached shells scattered throughout the field. Davidson observed that these shells were mostly the remains of oysters, and yet he knew there were no oyster beds in nearby Slaughter Creek, nor was it likely that there ever had been any. The nearest source for oysters, he was told, was in Delaware Bay, some three or four miles away. Thus it seemed clear that the oysters must have been gathered in the bay and transported up the navigable waters of Slaughter Creek to the village. He noted that the shells were concentrated in areas roughly circular or oval in shape, but conforming to no regular pattern. Between these areas there was only a slight sprinkling of shells or they were entirely absent. Davidson decided to explore the areas of shell concentration by digging into them to learn what lay beneath.

Scarcely had he begun to dig when he found that the shells strewn on the surface of the ground had been plowed out of deposits that extended deeper into the earth. It was obvious that the natives, several centuries before, must have dug sizable holes in the ground and then filled them with oyster shells. These holes varied in depth from three to eight feet and averaged six or eight feet in diameter. Davidson called these shell-filled holes "pits" and estimated that the site was pocketed with more than a hundred of them. A foot or more of topsoil had gathered on top of the pits, making a flat and relatively even surface, concealing their locations. But Farmer Jones, after many successive years of cultivating his fields, had plowed through the overlying humus and the plow blade gouged into the shells beneath, bringing them to the surface and scattering them over the field. Why or how the shells had been placed in the holes in the first place constituted the problem to be answered. With his student crew, reinforced by a few Delaware amateurs, and on several occasions assisted by boys employed on a local Civilian Conservation Corps drainage project whose officers had volunteered assistance, the anthropologist set to work unraveling the tangled threads of the archaeological mystery. With trowel, camel-hair brushes, and small digging tools, he began the tedious work of removing the shells from the pits, taking photographs and keeping detailed notes of each stage in the digging operations.

As work progressed, other materials in addition to the shells were encountered. Here and there in the pits, mixed with the shells, the diggers' trowels found pockets of charcoal, ashes, decayed vegetable matter blackened with age, charred wood fragments, and the bones of deer, bear, raccoon, squirrel, and wild turkey, as well as broken turtle shells and fish bones. At first the thought occurred that fires may have been lighted in the pits, since some of the shells were burnt and discolored by flame. But the theory was discounted when it was found that most of the shells had never been exposed to fire.

The pits also produced potsherds of all sizes, some burnt, others not touched by fire. Stone arrowheads, stone scrapers for removing flesh from animal pelts, bone needles used in net making, bone gorges used as fishhooks, bone awls, fragments of clay smoking pipes, hammerstones, celts, and other types of aboriginal implements were also unearthed. These materials were proved to be the handiwork of the native people who had dug the pits and filled them with the shells, and every specimen was carefully examined and studied in the hope of learning more about the former occupants.

The pottery fragments, which were of unusual interest, were

far more numerous than the sherds found by Leidy and Jordan years before in southern Delaware. In fact, several bushels of pot fragments were collected which originally had been parts of some two hundred clay vessels. After these fragments were cleaned, the students cemented together some of the pieces to effect partial restorations. Mr. Omwake, Archibald Crozier, and other members of the Archeological Society also troweled out large numbers of sherds from the shell pits and completely restored several vessels by fitting and cementing the pieces together. These restored vessels are now on exhibit at the Archaeological Museum in the University of Delaware. From examining the restored vessels and the hundreds of fragmentary rims and bottoms, it could be seen that the original pots varied in size from small cups to gallon-size containers, and had once been used as cooking vessels or water carriers. When compared to modern cooking vessels, these aboriginal pots seem very crude. The potter who made them, like all New World prehistoric peoples, knew nothing of the potter's wheel—or any kind of wheel for that matter—and the ware is illustrative of a primitive craft in which the human hands did the molding and the sun and campfires the baking. The color of the pottery, which was unpainted, was the natural yellow or red tint of the clay. The outer walls had a ribbed or roughened appearance, although the interior surface was smooth. The vessels tended to be straight-lipped, although a few had slight rims. The only decorations consisted of short, deep diagonal grooves, and triangle of herring-bone designs around the top of the pots. These designs had probably been made by etching the soft clay with a twig or bone splinter as an artistic expression of the potter.

The method used in the manufacture of the pottery as established by careful study of the sherds was the "coil technique" identical with the method used in making the pottery uncovered at Rehoboth in 1870 by Francis Jordan. In fact, the pottery was very similar in color, size, texture, and incising, which indicated a homogeneous cultural relationship between the Slaughter Creek people and those who had once camped at Rehoboth and Lewes. Thus by their pottery vessels one native group can be compared to another, even though living members of the tribe have long since passed out of the pages of history. The arrowpoints, scrapers, stone axes, and other implements and weapons made by the Slaughter Creek peoples were no different from those found at Lewes and Rehoboth, further accentuating the similarity between the prehistoric residents of the two areas. The reader must remember that these cultural materials differ greatly from similar objects found on prehistoric sites in New York, Pennsylvania, and elsewhere. In the shape and size of a pottery vessel, its ornamentation, the type of clay and tempering materials employed in its manufacture, the archaeologist is provided with a cultural yardstick. Likewise the shape of an arrowhead or a stone axe, the technique of manufacture, and the type of stone used in its construction, are often valuable clues to the identity of a tribe. Whereas the historian gathers his information from printed documents and records, the archaeologist must resort to the more subtle story told by stone and clay artifacts, shells, teeth, and bones. Inasmuch as it is characteristic of all communities, ancient and modern, to copy practices of their neighbors, the influence of one native group upon another has left its mark on their cultural properties.

On a hot Sunday in May 1934, Davidson and two of his students, Eiseley and Faust, with Omwake and Crozier, encountered a skeleton while digging test holes a few feet from the edge of one of the shell pits they had previously excavated. It proved to be the remains of a middle-aged female, buried about thirty-six inches below the surface of the ground. She had been interred in a partially dismembered condition, but with an attempted arrangement of the bones in their normal positions in the grave. The investigators concluded that the head and other members had been severed from the body before burial and the bones scraped free of flesh. Again we are confronted with evidence of the strange custom that has already been cited as characteristic of the mortuary practices of some of the southern Delaware tribes. There was nothing buried with the dead Indian woman, and any evidence of clothing, hair, and flesh had long since decayed. Nothing remained but her dry, yellowed bones, but to Davidson they were an invaluable source of data, and he uncovered them with utmost care.

The reader may be surprised to learn that from examining an individual's bones the anthropologist is able to determine the age, sex, height, and racial type of that individual; whether he was diseased or died from violent causes and whether he had any deformities. The age of the person is established through the number and condition of the teeth and the sutures in the skull which grow closer together with advanced years. Sex can be determined by observing the skull and pelvic construction. Moreover a typical female skeleton is less massive than the male. Other definite characteristics in the formation of bones and teeth enable the anthropologist to distinguish an Indian skeleton from those of a white person or Negro. The study of skeletal remains, called physical anthropology, is a highly specialized field of research, requiring skill in the use of instruments to measure the various bones in the human body and knowledge of the physical types of prehistoric man.

On October 7, 1934, another female skeleton was found during the excavation of a shell pit. One of the youthful CCC workmen, doing spade digging, had carelessly, and contrary to Davidson's instructions, dug outside of the perimeter of one of the pits under excavation. He brought up a large piece of human skull on his shovel. Davidson immediately called a halt to the use of the shovel and personally went to work with a trowel and brush to uncover the skeleton. It proved to be a flexed burial —the body had been interred with the knees drawn up to the abdomen in a sitting position. It, too, was a female burial, and like the first there had been no ornaments or utensils placed in the grave. Unlike the first skeleton, this one was completely articulated, and apparently the corpse had not been subjected to any bone-cleaning rites before burial. The woman had apparently been placed in the grave with care, perhaps dressed in her best deerskin skirt, of which nothing remained.

It proved to be a lucky day indeed for the archaeologists, because shortly after exhuming the second skeleton another grave was encountered. Unlike the first two, this grave contained the bones of three males. The remains had been completely cut apart before burial, and lay jumbled together in a careless heap. The three skulls were neatly placed on top of the pile of bones, an awesome sight to the CCC boys who crowded around the hole. A significant feature was that the three men had not been buried in a conventional grave, but had been laid to rest in one of the shell pits. Their bones were completely surrounded by waste shells, animal bones, and the usual detritus of the shell pit. Like the others, no ornaments or weapons had been buried with the bodies. In this group or "nested" burial, which differed from the former two interments, there were striking similarities to the ossuary uncovered at the Rehoboth bluff by Wigglesworth, although fifteen individuals had been buried at Rehoboth as contrasted to the three at Slaughter Creek. Nevertheless in both instances the bones had been dismembered before burial, suggestive of the bone-cleaning rites and ossuary burial already mentioned.

The three distinct types of burials at Slaughter Creek, namely, the first partially disarticulated skeleton, the second flexed skeleton, and the third group burial were indicative of three entirely different mortuary customs. Whether one type of burial, the flexed, for example, was an earlier custom which gave way to the adoption of other more recent customs, or whether all were contemporary could not be proved. Davidson tentatively concluded, however, that the flexed burial, known to be an old mode of Indian interment, was the original mortuary practice of the Slaughter Creek people, but that they had borrowed the other types of burial customs from more southerly peoples, among whom, as in Virginia and the Carolinas, the scraped bone and ossuary burial was a conventional practice. If true, this would indicate that Delaware's prehistoric peoples were being influenced by the customs of other tribes which had diffused to their region. Recognizing that it was necessary to uncover additional human remains to obtain sufficient data to permit valid conclusions to prove his point, Davidson recommended that a more extensive digging project be sponsored at Slaughter Creek. Unfortunately, for a number of reasons, this was never done.

One of the primary deterrents in permitting further excavation was the number of curiosity seekers who, spurred by the thought of finding Indian treasures, began to trespass on the site after learning that skeletons had been found. There followed individual and careless digging by vandals which was never recorded. The fields were overrun by persons seeking Indian relics, and the crops were trampled under their selfish feet. The owner of the property, whose livelihood depended upon cultivating his fields, deemed it proper to forbid further archaeological digging on the site. The matter might have been satisfactorily handled by an outright purchase of the land for scientific purposes, but there were no funds available for such acquisition.

In a scientific paper describing his preliminary work at Slaughter Creek, Davidson advanced the theory that the shell pits were originally intended as refuse or garbage pits. He believed that the Indians had gathered oysters in Delaware Bay, transporting them by canoe to their village via Slaughter Creek as an important element in their diet. We can assume that they indulged in great oyster feasts.

Although we have no direct evidence as to the habits of these Indians in policing their village [Davidson wrote], there are reasons for believing that the shells, possibly after each meal, were gathered into baskets or other containers and dumped into the pits. Shells usually free from much earth or other debris are often found solidly in spaces of a cubic foot or two as if dumped out of some container rather than tossed individually or in small groups into the pit. Alongside of such an accumulation or surrounded by several of them one occasionally finds others of approximately equal size consisting of a few shells mixed with charcoal and earth, fragments of animal bones, sherds of pottery, and occasionally a broken stone or bone artifact, as if representing the sweepings of a hearth gathered together in a basket for disposal in the pits.

Why the three dismembered skeletons with the skulls on top constituting the nested burial should have been interred in one of the refuse pits instead of in a conventional grave could not be fully explained, although, as we have seen, human remains were found by Leidy in the shell heaps at Lewes also surrounded by refuse. One might again speculate that death may have occurred at a time of the year when the ground was frozen and a grave was difficult to dig with the crude tools available to the villagers. Since the shell pit had been dug earlier in the season, it might thus have been conveniently utilized as a grave. The occupants may have considered it as respectable a burying place as any other hole in the ground.

The five skeletons were carefully studied by Dr. John Noon, one of Davidson's associates who prepared a scientific paper describing them. His measurements indicated that three of the individuals were long-headed, one broad-headed and the fifth was medium-headed. As future skeletons are uncovered in the state, these data will prove useful in arriving at conclusions relative to the physical types represented in Delaware. People of the same racial family tend to have heads that follow an average shape, and the presence of peoples of an alien type can often be detected by the shape of their skulls if a series is available. The older Algonkians are usually termed a "long-headed" people.

As to the identities of the natives who lived at Slaughter Creek, the utensils, implements, and pottery which had been unearthed held the answer. They were of the distinct type of artifact which archaeologists attribute to Indians of a woodland cultural pattern. In Delaware these woodland people were the forbears of the Algonkian-speaking Indians who greeted the first settlers, and for all we know they spoke the same language. They were no different in culture from the other native groups whose artifacts found throughout southern Delaware are identical in type. The Slaughter Creek inhabitants were a primitive hunting and fishing folk, and to them the latter pursuit was the more important, especially the gathering of oysters for food. That they erected small huts made of tree limbs and bark would be expected, although no evidence of these huts were located. This was perhaps due to the fact that the excavators were not seeking soil disturbances suggestive of house sites but were specifically concerned with investigating the problem of the shell pits. Inasmuch as no metal tools, iron, glass, or any materials of European manufacture were found, Davidson thought it safe to conclude that the occupants had never made contact with white settlers or traders and were indeed a truly prehistoric people. This must be qualified by explaining that the relatively well-advanced stages in their stone and clay industry would assign them to a very late prehistoric period, say somewhere between 1300 A.D. and 1600 A.D.—a far cry from the paleolithic man whose artifacts Hilborne Cresson claimed to have discovered at Claymont.

7.

Sussex Diggings

My own personal experiences in digging for traces of prehistoric man in Delaware began in 1937, the year I moved to Wilmington. Therefore the ensuing incidents can be related in the first person. They are not offered as reminiscences, for the episodes of which I write are not of the past but of today. Geiger Omwake and I are currently exploring the waterways of Delaware in our spare moments, seeking aboriginal sites, as we have done since we first met. Each trip brings new data for his map on which he is plotting the locations of ancient encampments in the state, a project of priceless value to future investigators in Delaware. In less than ten years he had accumulated more than fifteen thousand stone and clay artifacts, largely by surface hunting, which he recently presented to the Archaeological Museum at the University of Delaware. He has already covered more of Delaware on foot than most persons do in a lifetime, and knows the locations of almost two hundred prehistoric sites.

Two weeks before this chapter was written, my good friend Chan Robinson and I hiked through the country of the Murderkill River between Frederica and Killen's Mill Pond and in the fields along St. Jones Creek below Dover, searching for specimens of the early occupation that we knew had existed there. His remarkably interesting collection of several thousand stone and clay implements, all perfect, gathered on the surface of the ground in this vicinity during the last three decades, are the result of a boyhood curiosity that has never deserted him. And only last Saturday Archibald Crozier invited me to join him on a trip to the ancient sites at Hog Swamp in Newport and the old

Pordham Farm along White Clay Creek at Stanton, less than twenty minutes by car from downtown Wilmington. Twenty-five years ago he and Mrs. Crozier were regular callers at both places when, as springtime canoeists and members of the Wilmington Canoe Club, they paddled up the Christina River with the incoming tide, pausing on the way to browse through plowed fields in search of the implements of a forgotten people. Today as then, Arch is adding new specimens to his cabinet, and collectors yet unborn will undoubtedly follow in his footsteps on the identical sites and be rewarded in their quest. Truly it seems impossible to exhaust the supply of prehistoric materials that lie around us awaiting discovery. Far more interesting, of greater scientific value, and yet more difficult to fathom are the sub-surface clues. These must be probed, as Joe Wigglesworth learned, through the use of tools and excavational techniques.

My first digging in Delaware was within a few miles of my home on the old McDaniel farm lying opposite Newport between the Christina River and None Such Creek. Many stone specimens had been picked up on the surface in the fields along the streams, and it seemed possible that the soil might hold more of interest. Several Saturdays were spent here with spade and shovel assisted by the owner, Harry Spence, and some of his friends.

Next I turned to a little truck farm in Stanton near Red Clay Creek where the tenant farmer had plowed up a varied assortment of arrowheads, broken axes, and stone rejectage. After this I spent some time in Folly Woods on the western shore of the fishing pond which seemed promising. There, assisted by several friends, we unearthed a variety of stone objects from the humus. All three sites proved to be shallow, and the cultural materials were confined exclusively to the upper humus layer. The plow had uprooted everything of value on the first two sites, and below the plow line the red brick clay was hard and sterile, although we explored ten and twelve feet deep. This proved that the occupation had been of relatively short duration, probably the temporary camping places of huntsmen and fishermen. They apparently came for a short visit in late prehistoric times, then moved elsewhere, leaving only superficial deposits behind. Nothing was found even slightly suggestive of any great antiquity.

The first digging project which seems worthy of detailed note was at the Moore Shell Heap in Sussex County. Our first trip to the site was in 1939 in company with J. K. Spare of Moylan, Pennsylvania, his congenial wife and daughter, James Scott, L. T. Alexander, and the Delaware artist John Swientochowski, who is also a painstaking archaeologist. Mr. Spare deserves credit for having found the site, which lay on a canal running between Lewes and Rehoboth. He had been pleasure cruising through the canal when he noticed an unusual hummock along the bank. He went ashore to make an examination and saw that the rain had washed out some pottery fragments, shells, and the bones of a human skeleton. Realizing that he had encountered a station of possible archaeological value, Mr. Spare sought our assistance upon his return. We met at luncheon and planned a reconnaissance together.

The trip was one of many excursions to the site. After the first visit Mr. Spare, because of business obligations, was unable to participate further, and it fell largely upon John Swiento- chowski and me to carry through the project to completion. Mr. and Mrs. Moore, the owners of the property, were genial hosts, sympathetic with our mission, and after digging all day we usu- ally stayed overnight in their home, one of the typical cypress- shingled farmhouses of southern Delaware. The soft feather mattress of their spare bed and pillows stuffed with duckdown were fit for more royal heads than ours, and the food served by Mrs. Moore—fried chicken, home-made sausage cooked over a wood-burning stove and sweet potato pie browned in the oven —made our frequent visits exceptionally pleasant. In the quiet of the Sussex nights we chatted with our hosts by lamplight and enjoyed the rural relaxation that is never found in a city. From time to time we were accompanied and assisted by Archibald Crozier, Stanley Swientochowski, Ted Stern, a student in the Department of Anthropology at the University of Pennsylvania, Richard Stearns of the Maryland Natural History Society, and

Jake Moore, the affable son of the owner of the property, who occasionally gave us a hand with the heavy digging.

The Moore farm lies on the edge of a plateau which slopes down gradually behind the farmhouse and then dips abruptly to an extensive salt meadow used as pasture land. The meadow is bisected by the canal, a deep artificial cut, about thirty-five or forty feet wide. The canal, which is nine miles long, was opened in 1913 to connect Rehoboth Bay and Delaware Bay as part of an inland waterway to Chincoteague. The great expectation of water traffic never materialized, and today the waterway is used mainly by small pleasure craft. On the west bank of the canal a circular hummock about four feet high in the center and one hundred fifty feet in circumference made a conspicuous elevation in the low-lying meadow. As one looked down from the rear of the farmhouse the mound appeared to be a curious but seemingly natural promontory in which tufts of scrub grass and prickly pear cactus had taken root. On the eastern slope—the side facing the canal and laved by its waters—the surface sand had washed away, exposing thousands of white shells in the face of the mound. The sand mantle covering the hummock proved to be only a few inches thick, and when it was brushed aside the underlying shells were exposed. No matter where we dug in the mound, the spade was stopped by the thick deposit of shells beneath the sand.

Therefore we decided to begin our digging in the soft sand beyond the northern side of the mound. There we sunk a trench at right angles to the canal and extending along the entire northern slope of the hummock. The trench was twenty-five feet long, three feet deep, and three feet wide. By troweling against the vertical southern face of the trench, we advanced the entire cut forward, throwing the debris behind us, thus filling the trench as we advanced. It also permitted a cross-section view, or profile reading of the soil, as we sliced ahead. We divided the mound into theoretical ten-foot squares with numbered stakes, following an accepted technique, which would later permit us to plot our digging on a blueprint. Eventually, by inches, we completely dug down the entire mound, finishing up on the op-

Moore Shell Heap before and after the beginning of excavation

Fragments of rims of clay pottery vessels from the Moore Shell Heap

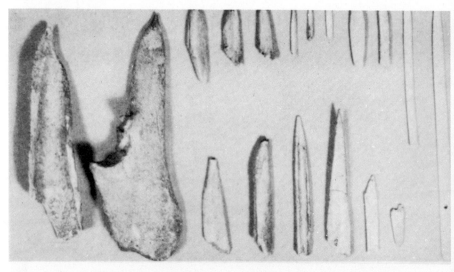

Awls, needles, bodkins and other tools made of animal bone excavated at Moore Shell Heap

posite side from where we had started, as one slices a loaf of bread from one crust to the other. The task required more than a year, and was done over week-ends, holidays, and vacation periods. Johnny took many photographs and measurements to illustrate the progressive stages in the work which now repose in the files of the Archaeological Society of Delaware.

"If I were getting paid for this," Johnny said to me one hot July day when we were digging in the heap, "there wouldn't be enough money in the world to keep me on the job." I agreed with him that only for a labor of love would two men willingly subject themselves to the punishment we suffered that summer. There were no trees in the lowland to shade us from the blazing sun, and our bodies always were wet with perspiration. To yield to the temptation to shed our shirts was to invite attack by deerflies, yellow-bodied pests that buzzed around our heads and stung like hornets when they landed. The damp meadow was also a breeding ground for mosquitoes, and in the morning they arose from the dewey grass and remained with us until midafternoon. Despite the heat I worked in an old felt hat pulled down over my ears, a bandanna around my neck and canvas gloves on my hands, so that no patch of skin would be exposed to attack. Johnny usually had a briar pipe in his mouth, puffing like a locomotive, the smoke screen around his head his only protection against the insects.

To add to our misery, now and then a strong gust of salt wind from the ocean would swirl up the canal, and in a few seconds our throats and noses were clogged with the fine ashes and dust of the excavated debris. At the end of a day's work we both looked like black-face comedians, and it required plenty of scrubbing in the metal basin under the pump in Mrs. Moore's wash-shed to remove the prehistoric crust from our bodies.

The Jersey cows grazing in the meadow were our only visitors, and they, too, became bothersome. The heifers evinced an insatiable curiosity in the project, and edged up until we were in the center of a semicircle of ruminating faces. We were afraid that one of the animals might fall into our trench and break a leg or cause the wall to cave in. Almost regularly on the hour,

Johnny would spring out of his burrow and run toward the cows, yelling and waving his spade.

"Vamoose! Go home!" he would shout as they almost broke their necks to escape the wrath of the fiend who pursued them. The husband of the herd discreetly kept his distance, but in the evening as we started back to the farmhouse he would block our path. With horns lowered, and anger seething in his red eyes he seemed to be daring us to come near. Good judgment being the better part of valor, and not wishing to become ourselves subjects for future archaeologists, we usually detoured through the marshes at the expense of getting mired from toe to thigh.

These annoyances were trivial when compared to the thrill of uncovering an object from the earlier culture. We soon discovered that the tools used in the domestic life of the builders of the shell mound were mixed with the dirt and refuse. Often we troweled for hours, finding only shells and ashes. Then suddenly one of us would let out a whoop as the end of a bone awl, netting needle, or some other artifact came into view in the vertical wall of the trench. Ten or fifteen tense minutes followed as we patiently uncovered the fragile object, holding our breaths for fear it might crumble to dust. After removing it and allowing it to lie in the sun, the moisture would evaporate and another century-old tool would be dry and hard and suitable for museum study and exhibition. There were innumerable false alarms to build up our hopes and then let us down. Occasionally we would see the surface of what appeared to be a human skull. After fifteen or twenty minutes of breathless work, it would turn out to be a piece of turtle shell browned with age. Then, again, a large piece of pottery would be seen, and as we tediously brushed away the surrounding dirt, exposing more and more, we were certain that we were on the verge of finding a complete vessel. But alas, it invariably would be only a fragment of a broken pot.

Slowly but surely our inventory of excavated materials increased, and we found many perfect specimens that alone were worth the efforts we expended in the information they conveyed. Arrowheads, scrapers, stone chips, potsherds, bone tools, hammerstones, stone drills, ornaments, a piece of turtle-shell drinking cup, a clam-shell spoon, and others were added to our collection. One of the most interesting tools was a large awl made from the heelbone of an elk, the joint of the bone constituting a natural handle. By the time the project was completed we had gathered 415 potsherds of varying sizes and several hundred bone and stone artifacts. Unfortunately no additional trace of human remains was found. Apparently there had been only one skeleton in the heap which had previously been washed out by the rains.

＊　　＊　　＊

One day during the spring plowing, a sudden rainstorm interrupted our digging in the shell heap and we hurriedly sought shelter in the farmhouse.

After about three hours the rain subsided, but the earth was too muddy to permit further digging that day. Jake Moore had been plowing in one of the adjacent fields before the storm, and we decided to take a walk and see if he had turned up anything of archaeological interest. We splashed through the pasture separating us from the field, and scrambled over the barbed-wire fence. There we were confronted with an unusual sight that we will never forget. The rain had beaten down so hard that the tracks of the tractor and the plow furrows were almost completely obliterated. Scattered over the muddy field were approximately fifty circular areas where the earth was stained a deep red in color. Each area was about six feet in diameter, and they occurred throughout the field in no recognizable pattern. The ground between these red splotches was the natural gray of the sandy loam. We lost no time in investigating one of the red-stained areas, and within its perimeter found the soil heavily laden with ashes, charcoal, aged animal and fish bones, burnt shells, and stones cracked from heat which had been plowed out of the soil before the storm. The other reddened areas were identical with the first, and in some of them we picked up an assortment of burnt potsherds and animal bones. For a few moments we were puzzled. Then the explanation dawned upon us.

We were viewing the remains of campfires, not of recent origin, but fires that had burnt in the past. They had obviously burnt many times to make such deep and permanent stains in the earth. We were extremely fortunate to have stepped into the field when an ideal combination of freshly upturned dirt and a driving rain permitted us the rare view. We questioned Jake Moore and he said he had never seen anything like it before, although he had cultivated the field for several seasons. The next day when the sun had dried the earth, the discoloration had strangely disappeared and the soil was uniform in color throughout the field. We should have had difficulty locating the fired areas if we had not previously marked several of them with stakes.

Later we made test diggings in the field, excavating in the marked areas, and also in the intervening soil. Our theories were confirmed that this was the major place of occupation, the true village of the aborigines who had been responsible for the near-by shell heap. As we troweled into the earth we found a number of post-molds—discolorations in the ground—the remains of posts long since decayed which we recognized as the marks of the upright corner poles of aboriginal huts. These post-molds were in the soil, beneath the humus, immediately behind the fire-stained areas, indicating that a fireplace had been built in front of each hut. Although we were forced to confine our efforts on the main site to test pitting because it was such an extensive area, nevertheless many interesting specimens were found, including a stone gorget, celt, pestle, several axes, stone hoe, bone implements, and a very large quantity of potsherds. Undoubtedly there is a burial ground near-by or even an ossuary, perhaps within the bounds of the village that may be discovered in the future, but we were unable to locate it in our limited digging.

Without burdening the reader with details relating to all of the digging procedures we employed, let us pass on to what we believe is a plausible theory after analyzing our data.

Sometime prior to 1600—how many years before we could not be certain—a community of prehistoric fishermen and farmers developed on the plateau that is now the Moore farm. The field in which we found the fireplaces was only a portion of the village, for we were certain that the Moores' house, barn, and other farm buildings also covered some of the original site. This high sandy terrain provided excellent drainage and was well protected from floods, high tides, and ocean storms. From near-by springs gushed an ample supply of fresh drinking water. A creek flowed through the marsh that separated the plateau from Delaware Bay, and this stream, navigable by canoe, was the convenient avenue used by the villagers to go back and forth to their fishing and oystering haunts in the bay.

A pine forest had once covered the plateau, but the natives burned down some of the trees to make cleared land for their huts and gardens. Since the village was intended as a permanent dwelling place, they erected sturdy huts with upright corner posts well anchored in the soil. These huts were no doubt similar to those seen by the early colonists, who have described them as being square or rectangular with arched roofs, thatched on the outside with bark and dried-grass mats, and lined on the inside with grass and cornhusks. The hut had no doors or windows except a single opening, covered with an animal skin, by which the occupants entered. The only furniture in the hut was a wooden bench built along one of the sides, covered with straw and animal skins. This served as a bed for all the family, and beneath it was a storage place for clothing, firewood, and other necessities. A hole was left in the roof, and in the winter a fire was built on the ground in the center of the hut, the smoke escaping through the roof. In the summer larger fires were built outside the huts. The hut gave protection from the summer sun and rain as well as the cold blasts and winter snows. There were probably twenty-five or thirty identical huts in the village, each one housing a separate family.

The soil surrounding the huts was very fertile, and each family had its own garden. While the men fished, the women planted corn, beans, tobacco, and pumpkins, cultivating the soil with digging sticks and stone hoes. We excavated the remains of corn that had become carbonized, and bean pods which had turned black from age but had withstood disintegration by being protected in the soil against air and moisture.

During the fishing season the men paddled down to the bay in their dugouts made from hollowed logs, gathered oysters, clams, or conches, and fished in the waters with nets and with grass and sinew lines to which bone hooks were fastened. When they returned to the village the oysters were shucked, then dried for winter use by exposing them to smoke from the open fires which burned outside the houses. The fish were cleaned and also dried for winter use by first gutting them and then spreading them in the sun.

Almost all of the stone implements used by these villagers and other southern Delaware natives were made from pebbles and boulders deposited by glacial out-wash or of marine origin. There are no stone cliffs or rock outcroppings in this flat sandy country which could be quarried for suitable stone. Thus the procurement of the proper kind of stone was a serious economic problem. We found a few arrowheads made of rhyolite, argillite, shale, and other exotic stones which would indicate that the villagers either traveled great distances to obtain the stone material or traded with northern and western peoples who lived in regions where suitable stone was more readily accessible.

Because of this scarcity of native stone, one is led to suppose that many tools and implements were made of wood. Unfortunately wood perishes rapidly in the Delaware soil, so the archaeologist must resort to speculation when he attempts to picture all the artifacts in use. Among those made of wood, some of which have been mentioned, there were probably included net floats, clubs, wedges, handles for knives, axes, and scrapers, arrowshafts, bows, and bowls. There were doubtless many others.

In stone-working, the artisan's tools consisted of hammerstones, bone flaking tools, and abrading or rubbing stones. A large pebble could be converted into a hoe blade, net sinker, axe, or celt by pecking at it with a hammerstone to bring it down to the desired shape. The encircling groove in a stone axe for fastening the handle was also cut into the stone by carefully tapping it with the hammerstone, thus dislodging small particles. The cutting edge was made by rubbing it with a sandy abrading stone. Often the entire surface of an axe or celt was thoroughly abraded, which gave the implement a smooth, highly polished surface. Arrowheads, scrapers, drills, knives, and spearpoints were made by reducing suitable pebbles to the desired shape by striking them repeatedly with a hammerstone. Then by skilfully exerting pressure to its edges with a bone tool, flakes were thrown off and the object gradually took shape. Finally, tiny chips were flaked off the edges to make it sharp. Some of the larger flakes were also sharpened by retouching their edges with the flaking tool, thus making handy cutting tools. No fire was used in making arrowheads and other chipped implements, as has often been thought. The most important thing, in addition to the skill necessary to exert proper pressure with the flaking tool, was in the selection of the type of flinty stone that responded to chipping without breaking. John Swientochowski is one of a number of modern students who have patiently developed a genuine skill in stone working and can fashion an arrowhead, using aboriginal methods, within a few minutes.

To make a hole in a flat stone ornament, or other thin stone object, the natives resorted to the use of a stone drill. It was fastened to the end of a shaft as an arrowhead would be attached. Then the shaft was twisted in the bowstring and by sawing the bow back and forth the drill revolved and penetrated the surface to be perforated. Holes in shell beads could be made by using the same technique.

Holes in thicker stone objects were made by using hollow reeds in conjunction with fine sand. The sand was placed on the stone to be perforated, then the end of the hollow reed was revolved back and forth on the loose sand. The sand acted as an abrasive to cut into the stone, while the reed was the instrument to apply the friction. To facilitate the task, the driller usually made the hole halfway through the stone, then he turned it over and started another hole on the opposite side. Finally the two holes met in the center, as an examination of a reed-drilled object will clearly show.

So far as the domestic life of the people is concerned, they apparently were able to fill all their needs from their natural environment. They probably made baskets of oak splints, and bags by weaving dried marsh grass. Such containers were needed in transporting the great quantities of clams and oysters to their village, and also for carrying vegetables. Their smoking pipes, cooking vessels, and water containers were molded from clay, and in view of the huge quantities of sherds that remained on the site one surmises that each family group was well supplied with pottery ware. The presence of many sherds also implies advanced culinary arts, and stews and soups made from fish and vegetables may have been a staple part of their diets. Such food could have been served in wooden dishes and eaten with clamshell spoons.

These natives stews, soups, roasts, and barbecues would not be very palatable to us because they apparently were very greasy and lacked the flavor of salt. The bread which the women made from corn meal and the ash cakes baked in the hot coals were eaten without benefit of butter, and we would consider them soggy and unsatisfying. These villagers also ate animals and fowl, as shown by the presence of bird and mammal bones in their refuse; but the predominating item in their diet was shellfish. Edible berries, roots, and fruits growing wild in the neighboring woods were probably gathered by the women and children in season.

In the fall, the men no doubt went into the woods to hunt deer, elk, bear, wolves, and other animals primarily to obtain furs for winter clothing. The women scraped the flesh from the animal skins with stone scrapers and stretched them on wooden frames, rubbing the animal's brain into the pelt to make it soft.

To describe the appearance of the people one must rely solely on imagination in the absence of archaeological data. However, guided by the notes of some of the early explorers in the Delaware Valley it seems safe to risk a few brief comments. Let us introduce one of the typical fishermen of the village. He is of average height, legs slightly bowed, strong arms and muscular shoulders. He has a straight nose, broad cheekbones, dark eyes that are almond shaped, and a complexion the color of cinnamon. He is smooth-shaven and has also removed most of the hair from his long head by cutting it off with a sharpened stone flake. He has allowed a crest of hair to remain in the center of his head growing from the crown all the way back to the nape of his neck. His clothing in summer consists of three pieces, a pair of moccasins made from deer or elk hide, and a breechclout of the same material. He has smeared smelly bear grease on his legs and arms to keep mosquitoes away. Around his neck he wears a leather pouch on a thong which contains his stone knife, tobacco, bone fishhooks, and other possessions.

His wife is not as tall, but her complexion is the same color as his, and she has the same wide high cheeks and narrow eyes. She has plaited her hair in long braids and oiled it with raccoon grease to make it glisten. She wears a short deerskin skirt that reaches to her knees. She wears nothing above her waist except a string of shell beads around her throat. Her legs are bare and her feet are covered with moccasins made from braided corn husks. When she is working around her hut or in the garden she goes barefoot. In the winter, the couple will wear long deerskin leggings to cover their legs and thighs, and long tunics of bearskins fastened over one shoulder to protect their bodies.

The woman is the man's companion in marriage. She serves him obediently and bears his children. He provides for her and protects her against harm. Contrasted to modern civilizations, they lead a simple life as children of nature, eating, sleeping, fishing, planting, and breeding. They and their neighbors are peaceful folk. They seek no conquests and have few unfilled ambitions.

❁   ❁   ❁

By resorting to imagination to fill the empty pages, we have a fairly comprehensive story of the plateau village, even though it is of necessity incomplete in all details. What of the shell mound on the canal over which Johnny and I had so arduously labored? What was its purpose and how was it built? Through our digging, we learned that it had formerly been a sandy knoll on the bank of the little stream that meandered through the marshes down to the bay. The marsh had since dried up, forming the low meadow. The bed of the little stream is now inundated by the canal. One of the native families, we surmised, moved down to this knoll to live. Its size precluded the accommodation of more than one family. Perhaps this particular family group was unsocial, preferring to live apart from the main village. Or they may have decided that it would not be necessary to transport their supply of oysters all the way to the village, if they lived on a knoll more accessible from the stream. As the man of the house, if we may so designate him, returned each night with his boatload of oysters and clams, they were lifted out of the boat and piled in front of the hut. Later they were shucked, his wife and children assisting in the task. Some of the oysters and clams were eaten raw. Others were smoked to dry them, and stored away for use during the winter. The ashes and charcoal we excavated in the heap were all that remained of the fires, but were definite proof that fires had once burned. The useless shells were cast aside with the other refuse, the demolished pottery, the broken household utensils, and the fishing implements which we had uncovered.

Tragedy visited this little family group when their provider died from causes that are now unknown. He was buried in the hummock in front of his house, under the piles of discarded shells. His widow and children moved away, probably returning to the main village to live with the others. They left behind on the hummock the accumulations of the season, and the single corpse whose soul had gone to the Great Spirit.

The major question that confronts us is who specifically were the inhabitants of the village? Undoubtedly they were culturally related to Dr. Davidson's Slaughter Creek fishing folk, and to the fishermen who had encamped at Lewes and Rehoboth. The obvious similarity in their mode of living, as revealed by their artifacts, pottery, and shell refuse, permits this conclusion. While truly in a stone age, they were in a relatively late prehistoric period approaching the age of metal. We also assume that they were the forbears of the Algonkian-speaking Indians who lived in southern Delaware when the white men first settled in the region. If forced to name a date we would say they probably occupied the village between 1300 and 1600 A.D., and therefore were relatively recent occupants. We found no evidence to indicate that they had been preceded in the village by people of an older culture. The soil beneath their layer of occupation, which we also tested, bore no traces of man or animal.

* * *

Another jaunt to Sussex County with spade and trowel resulted from an unexpected telephone call one day from Philadelphia. The caller identified himself as Mr. I. L. Gordon, a business man associated with the Reading Terminal. He went on to say that while on a vacation trip to Rehoboth Beach a few weeks before, he had found what he surmised to be an Indian burial ground. At least, some boys told him they had been digging for Indian graves and had showed him where they claimed to have uncovered a skeleton. Immediately following his return to Philadelphia, Mr. Gordon had occasion to go to Washington on business, and while in the capital he stopped at the Smithsonian Institution to visit Dr. T. Dale Stewart, Curator of Physical Anthropology of the United States National Museum, appointed to succeed the late Aleš Hrdlička. Dr. Stewart, whose special field is the study of the skeletal remains of prehistoric peoples, consented to come to Rehoboth to investigate, and suggested that Mr. Gordon get in touch with me to ask if I would join them. "Did I care to accompany them?" Mr. Gordon asked. The answer was an emphatic affirmative.

The trip materialized over a week-end in June 1942. Mr. Gordon proved to be a courteous and hospitable guide, and early on Saturday morning we were driving in his car over a narrow unpaved cart road through the pine trees in a thickly wooded section a few miles south of Rehoboth Beach. Dr. Stewart was with us, and we were also accompanied by Mr. W. S. Corkran of Rehoboth, another of Mr. Gordon's friends. We emerged from the pine woods at the terminus of the Lewes-Rehoboth canal in a sandy clearing on an island overlooking the broad expanse of

Rehoboth Bay. Mr. Gordon pointed out the supposed burial ground on a high point of land, as he turned the car off the cart road and we bounced through the field. As we neared the site, the terrain became so uneven that he was compelled to stop the car, and we covered the remaining hundred yards on foot. There we found ourselves on top of what should be more properly termed a rise of land than a hill, because this entire coastal country is flat and devoid of hills. The crest of the land was overgrown with grass and weeds and had not been cultivated for several seasons, although it had formerly been used as farmland. We marveled at the beautiful view of the surrounding country—the wind-swept bay to the south and east, and the ragged green curtain of pine woods behind us. According to the pattern of aboriginal village sites in Delaware, the location seemed ideal as a place of habitation.

There were half a dozen scars in the field where the boys had apparently been digging at random for Indian graves, a pastime that should definitely have been discouraged by their elders. In the loose dirt near one of the depressions there were scattered fragments of bleached bones which Dr. Stewart immediately identified as human remains. It was easy to see that since the digging had been unscientific, this was another instance where human remains had been mutilated by untrained persons.

Dr. Stewart, who is both a physician and an anthropologist, examined the bones minutely. He told us that he had been gathering data relating to the spread of syphilis among the American Indians. In the late stages of the disease, the bones of the victim become pitted, and through an examination of the skeletal remains it is possible to detect these ineffaceable marks. He told us that for many years he had been seeking positive data that the disease was or was not present among American natives in prehistoric times. If affirmative data could be produced in skeletal material, it would tend to disprove the popular theory that syphilis was not known in America until it was brought by white explorers and illicitly transmitted to Indian women.

I reminded Dr. Stewart of the deposition made by one of the Dutchman during the settlement period who claimed that the explorers who landed at Lewes contracted syphilis from carousing with the Indian women who lived in a near-by village. While this testimony, if true, is not conclusive proof that the disease was present in America before the coming of the whites, Dr. Stewart agreed that the historical citation suggested that a study of prehistoric skeletons found in the Lewes-Rehoboth region might shed more light on the question. Therefore, he had a special interest in finding human skeletons in this particular region.

We had only two days at our disposal, and decided that the quickest method of procedure was to dig a series of test holes with the hope that we might find a grave through trial and error. The reader must not gather the impression that test holes are carelessly dug and that any kind of hole made in the ground will suffice. Test holes must be made carefully, allowing sharp vertical walls, for thorough examination. The major purpose of a test hole is to expose the underlying soil to scrutiny and not actually to dig into a grave. Breaking through a grave wall with a spade or shovel will often crush the bones and derange them, which is highly undesirable and destructive. It should again be emphasized that untrained persons should not attempt to excavate for Indians remains because they are not familiar with proper digging techniques and inevitably destroy valuable data.

We test-pitted first on the northern and eastern slope of the site without success, digging fifteen or twenty separate holes and filling them again. This consumed most of the morning. In the afternoon we turned our attention to the southern side of the site. The first spadeful of dirt which Dr. Stewart brought up contained shells and black soil which we recognized as having come from a disturbed area in the ground. We carefully laid back the humus with our spades to define the limits of the disturbed area, which was oval in shape, about five feet long and three feet wide in the center. Then we laid aside our spades, and went to work on our knees with trowels. We sliced down horizontally into the disturbed patch, carefully lifting out each trowelful of soil. At the depth of two feet our trowels at last struck bone, and we felt certain that we had reached a human grave. As we uncovered more of the bones, it became apparent that the skeleton lying buried was smaller than an adult, and we assumed that it might be the remains of a child.

We troweled and brushed most of the afternoon. Late in the day when the task was finished, we found that we had exposed not human remains but the skeleton of a dog. The bones were old and friable, and the animal belonged to a small species about the size of a fox terrier. The bones were articulated at the time the dog was buried, and the animal was placed on the floor of the grave on his side. In the soil surrounding the dog's skeleton we unearthed a number of oyster shells, charcoal fragments, potsherds, and the section of the stem of an ancient clay smoking pipe, similar to pipe fragments found elsewhere in southern Delaware. We were not certain that this material had been placed with the dog as grave goods, although it was possible that it had. As we completed our work on the dog grave, it began to grow dusky, and so, with aching backs, we filled the hole and returned to Rehoboth. Dr. Stewart and Mr. Gordon stayed overnight at Mr. Corkran's home, while I took advantage of the opportunity to drive over to Oak Orchard to spend the night with one of my Nanticoke Indian friends. I asked some of the Nanticokes whether their ancestors took any special pains in burying their dead dogs, but they could give me no useful information.

The next morning Stewart, Gordon, and I returned to the site, still puzzling over the significance of the dog burial, which was unlike anything that had been previously excavated in Delaware. We again resumed our test-pitting, and within an hour we located another disturbed area a few feet from the hole we had filled the previous evening. This time, it was I who was lucky enough to strike the black pay dirt. We again went to work with our trowels, and at a depth of about two and one-half feet encountered the remains of a second dog, of the same apparent species as the first. The bones were accompanied by shells and half a dozen unrelated red and yellow potsherds. These sherds were similar in structure and markings to the pottery Johnny and I had unearthed on the Moore village site, and to the pottery uncovered at Slaughter Creek. These seemed to indicate that the Rehoboth natives who had buried the dogs were of the same cultural horizon as those who occupied the two former sites. The dog bones were later examined by paleontologists at the Smithsonian Institution who pronounced them several hundred years old, although it was impossible to assign an exact date to them. The sandy soil covering the site is very dry and provides excellent drainage. Thus the rains are prevented from soaking into the earth and causing rapid decay of bone materials. With a skeleton so well protected against exposure to air and water, it would be entirely possible for it to lie in the earth for a thousand years or more without disintegrating. This is, of course, not true of bones which are buried in moist earth where decay is accelerated by the dampness. In some of the dry caves in the Southwest, feathers and baskets in an excellent state of preservation are found in graves known to be thousands of years old. Yet in low and exceedingly damp regions of the East, bodies buried in the soil for twenty-five years have often completely disintegrated.

We were still unable to explain the dog burials. We speculated that the graves may originally have been pits dug by the aborigines for the disposal of refuse, and that the dogs were buried intrusively in them after the animals had died naturally. It also occurred to us that perhaps the dogs had been sacrificed and buried ceremoniously as part of a native religious rite. We were well aware that many primitive peoples hold their dogs in great reverence. But the day closed with the question still unsettled, and since time was limited we could not continue with the work.

"Too bad you fellows didn't find any syphilitic human bones," Mr. Gordon said with a twinkle in his eye as we drove back to Rehoboth, "but maybe you have located the remains of a mysterious tribe of prehistoric dog worshippers." We all enjoyed a hearty laugh, but neither Dr. Stewart nor I had any better explanation to offer. We were certain only that the dog remains were prehistoric, and that they had been intentionally placed there by the members of a tribe who lived either on the site or not far distant.

*   *   *

Exactly two years elapsed before another visit could be made to the island in Rehoboth Bay. Those of us who follow archaeology as an avocation must not permit it to interfere with the obligations of our vocations, and time and distance are the main factors in limiting our activities. A week's vacation at Rehoboth Beach in June 1944 at last provided the opportunity to revisit the site. Kenneth Givan, one of the members of the Archaeological Society living at Lewes, offered to assist in the investigation, and his services were cheerfully accepted. Givan also faces the ever-present problem of finding leisure time to ride his hobby. A civil engineer by profession, he became an innkeeper a few years ago, and with his charming wife operates a now-famous travelers' lodge and restaurant near Lewes. He made the transition from plumb bob and transit to rolling pin and chafing dish with the greatest of ease. Having at various times eaten of the steamed Delaware Bay lobsters, soft shell crabs, and snapper soup, I can vouch for his knowledge of how to prepare dishes known also to the Indians. The lure of Delaware archaeology makes fellow travelers of men in such diverse professions as Dr. Joseph Leidy, a parasitologist; Francis Jordan, an importer; Joseph Wigglesworth, a city employe; Archibald Crozier, a credit manager; L. T. Alexander, an advertising executive; Harold Purnell, a hardware dealer; Geiger Omwake, a teacher; John Swientochowski, an artist; Arthur Volkman, a railroad clerk; Harold Lang, manager of a rug-cleaning establishment, and many others.

Givan, declaring a holiday from his kitchen, mustered together two young fellows to assist with the spadework, and we set out for the site. There, only a few miles from the vacationists splashing in the surf of the bay, we found the scars of the pits where Dr. Stewart and I had excavated the dogs. Apparently no one had been digging since our last visit. We resumed the test-hole technique in the same vicinity. Ten or fifteen test pits were sunk in the ground before we found an unmistakable disturbance in the soil—the signpost of archaeology—that told us we had again struck "pay dirt."

The disturbance continued down into the sandy subsoil, and at a depth of thirty inches we reached bone—not dog bone this time, but a human femur, the long bone of the leg. It was already too late in the day to uncover the rest of the skeleton which we hoped lay beneath us, and we filled the hole with loose sand until the next day.

The following morning was spent widening the test pit, encompassing a circular area eight feet in diameter and eighteen inches deep, with a sharp vertical wall around the entire perimeter to permit careful inspection of the soil. As we troweled deeper into the disturbance we found three human teeth, small molars from a child's jaw, and fragments of badly disintegrated bone. Our hopes fell, for it began to look as though someone had dug there previously and mutilated whatever the grave contained. But we continued with the work, hoping for the best.

Then deeper in the deposit we exposed a skull, then another, and still another. Between these crania, and on top and underneath them, were arm bones, leg bones, and vertebrae lying helter-skelter. By now we were positive that the grave had not been subjected to previous digging, yet the derangement of the bones was most puzzling. Then the explanation dawned on us which we might have guessed from the first. Through sheer accident we had troweled into one of the ossuaries similar to the grave excavated by the late Joe Wigglesworth near Rehoboth many years ago. Now it had been our privilege to examine an undisturbed ossuary with the bones still lying in their original positions.

Digging continued for several days as we carefully exposed the grave, being careful not to move any of the bones. We saw that the grave had been made in the shape of a rectangular trench, running east and west, three feet in width and not less than nine feet long. There, jumbled in the trench only a little over two feet from the surface of the ground were the skulls of eighteen persons—men, women, and children. Some were complete and in a fair state of preservation; others were badly disintegrated with parts missing. The skulls lay in a bed of human bones—ribs, legs, arms, and other bones crossing over and under in a crazy-quilt fashion. Some of the skulls lay face down; others were on their sides; and a few were placed in the earth upright.

The appearance and position of the skulls and bones indicated they had been carelessly placed in the trench grave, with no regard for arrangement. It was further apparent that many of the skulls and bones had been broken during or before burial, and that the bones had been separated from their natural positions on the bodies.

Scattered here and there were particles of charcoal, but the grave walls bore no indication of having contained a fire. In the southeast corner, however, a handful of burnt human bones and a small quantity of fine gray ashes were found in a little pocket. They had obviously been burnt before interment in the pit.

One piece of pottery, a thick red sherd about three inches square, lay with the bones in the center of the ossuary. Elsewhere we unearthed a broken argillite arrowpoint and three pieces of copper turned green from age. The metal was native American copper, beaten flat with a stone hammer, and rolled and twisted to form three tubular-shaped beads, each approximately an inch long. This we knew was the first authenticated record of copper artifacts excavated in the state since the days of Dr. Leidy and Francis Jordan. Needless to say we were thrilled, even though the beads were far from being classed as beautiful specimens. In fact, their workmanship was pitifully crude, but to the natives, ownership of the rare metal may have been a sign of affluence, and it was unquestionably a rare acquisition.

We could not determine whether the potsherd, arrowhead, and beads had been placed in the ossuary as accompaniment for the bones or whether they had accidentally found their way into the grave when it was filled. The beads lay alongside an isolated finger bone, which had been discolored green by the action of the copper salts, but they could not be definitely oriented as having been attached to a hand or wrist, although this possibility cannot be discounted. Chipped flakes of jasper and chert were

Uncovering the bones of 18 skeletons in the ossuary near Rehoboth Beach. The first layer has been exposed, showing disarticulated bones; the underlying layer proved to be a compact stratum of human bones.

Indians gathering oysters for winter use. The two women in the foreground are opening oysters and placing meat in clay vessels. The woman beside the hut is stringing oysters to suspend over fire to dry.

present in the sand covering the bones, proving that the manufacture of stone tools was practised on the site.

Assuming that the bones found in the ossuary had originally
been cut apart, scraped of their flesh and laid away in a chiacason house, as described in an early chapter, we can hazard a
reconstruction of the probable sequence of events. When time
came for the natives of the island village to hold one of their
periodic reburial ceremonies, they gathered together all of the
bones from the chiacason house, which was not far distant. The
bones of those who had been dead longest were obviously partially disintegrated from exposure to the air, while the bones of
the most recently deceased were still in an excellent state of
preservation. Thus some of the former remains were damaged
in the handling. A trench was dug with sharpened wooden sticks
or shells—a not too difficult task in the soft sand—of such a size
as to accommodate all the remains in the least possible space.
Then the bones were carried to the open grave from the chiacason house either by hand or in baskets, and indiscriminately
placed in the hole. From the broken condition of some of the
bones, they appear to have been thrown into their final resting
place with no regard for breakage.

Simultaneously, we can imagine, a fire or fires were lighted on
the surface of the ground near the open grave, the light casting
eerie reflections on the waters of the bay. Around the fire the
celebrants danced, observing their traditional ceremonial rites.
The highlight of the ceremony was a cremation—either of some
of the bones of one of the previously deceased, or by the sacrifice
of a living person. We cannot be certain of either, but we have
the authority of Captain John Smith's statement that some of the
Virginia tribes sacrificed a child each year by fire as part of one
of their sacred ceremonies. This point remains to be clarified,
but in other ossuaries charred bones are frequently uncovered,
suggestive of a human sacrifice.

The cremated bones and ashes were brushed together, probably with a sacred broom made from the wing of a wild turkey,
and carefully placed together in a little heap in the ossuary along
with the other bones. Finally the grave was filled with sand, and

we suspect that a small mound of earth remained to mark the
location, but it was eventually leveled off by weathering.

Why was the ceremony held? What was its significance? Why
were the bones preserved in the chiacason house? Why were
they scraped clean of flesh? Why were the bones reburied in a
common ossuary? Who were the people who participated in this
strange ritual? These are questions we were unable to answer,
and the possibility that the soil may hold the answer is the in-
centive that coaxes us on to further work.

We removed as many of the skulls as we could, along with
representative long bones, and sent them to Dr. Stewart at the
Smithsonian for study and as data to be used in the preparation
of a scientific report on the excavation.*

We refilled the burial pit, after first placing a permanent bench
mark in the center, and taking measurements which will enable
us to resume work as time and circumstances permit. We know
that more data await us in the soil of the island, and little by little,
as circumstances permit, we may be able to find the missing
links.

As we packed the bones in containers and carefully stowed
them in my car, Ken Givan urged us on.

"We are late," he said, "I must hurry home to bake a cake for
dinner."

*   *   *

While I was gathering notes in the field for *Delaware's Forgotten Folk*, my mentor, Dr. Frank Speck, the noted ethnologist,
frequently went with me to Indian River Hundred in Sussex
County. These visits among our living Nanticoke Indian friends
left little time for research among their dead ancestors, although
now and then we managed to devote a Sunday afternoon hunting for Indian darts in the near-by fields. Speck is well informed
on the trees, birds, and plant life and, quite apart from archaeology, our jaunts through the countryside were intensely interest-

---

* Dr. Stewart has recently informed me that he found no traces of syphilis on
the skulls from the ossuary. Preliminary examination also indicates that these
people were "long-headed."

ing and educational. Through his eyes I was privileged to witness the natural wonders of Delaware as they exist today, which, needless to say, one has a tendency to overlook as he probes into the past.

One Sunday afternoon in June, after exploring the furrows of the Puddle Hole Farm on Indian River, where we found several white quartz arrowheads, a hammerstone, and a notched pebble once used as a net sinker, we strolled down the river bank toward the inlet. We crossed through a woods and waded a little creek, stopping while Speck caught a blue-bellied lizard which the Nanticokes call a scorpion lizard, which was sleeping on a fallen gum log. Leaving the woods, we sloshed through a marsh where the ethnologist pointed out tracks like the imprint of a tiny human hand where a possum had come out of the woods to drink at one of the little runs. We continued along a narrow path which ended at a barbed-wire fence. As we climbed over this barrier into the meadow beyond, a pair of doves sunning themselves on the fence post took to the air.

On the far side of the meadow, on a crest of land which arose from the river bank, stood a house—an old early Virginian type of brick dwelling erected in 1722 by Woolsey Burton. His body, and the graves of other more recent Burtons, lay in a little walled graveyard at the west end of the house. Known throughout the Hundred as the White House, the dwelling was then occupied by Anthony Higgins, the writer, and his family.

We knew Tony as a keen student of Delaware history, especially well posted on the affairs, both past and present, of the Indian River country, so we availed ourselves of the unexpected opportunity to pay him a call. We started up the meadow, but before reaching the house we hailed Tony and his neighbor Jim Prettyman heading for the river. They waited for us, and we shook hands and chatted together for a few minutes. We saw that they were making preparations to go sailing on the river, and, in fact, Tony asked us if we cared to join them. When we explained that we were taking advantage of a few leisure hours to search for evidence of early Indian camps and villages, both young men pricked up their ears.

"Let's do it by boat," Tony said. "That's the way the Indians traveled, isn't it? Maybe you'll have better luck exploring by water than by land."

"Sure thing," Jim put in, always eager for adventure, "we weren't going to sail anywhere in particular. Let's join forces and hunt Indian relics. It's a new experience for me, but I'm willing to learn."

No further persuasion was needed. Fifteen minutes later the four of us were on our way up the river in the sloop, with Tony and Jim handling the sails and tiller, while Speck and I kept a sharp lookout along the shoreline for topographical features which seemed to hold promise. Early Indian sites in Delaware, as already pointed out, are usually found on sandy knolls or bluffs at the junction of a small tributary with the main river. It was a task to keep our eyes from wandering away from the shore, however, because never before in our excursions on foot along the banks had we seen anything to compare with the beauty of Indian River as viewed from the stream itself. It is beyond question Delaware's most scenic waterway. From our position in midstream we could look back at the sun shimmering on the rolling waters of the majestic inlet and the ocean beyond. Ahead of us, the river narrowed as it rippled along quietly through sandy farmland interspersed with woods of shadowy spruce, dogwood, and loblolly pine. The buzzards circling over the pines seem a permanent part of the landscape, and we counted more than fifty in the air at one time. Occasionally a silver flash appeared on the blue water as a bass splashed out to catch an insect. A fish-hawk hanging almost motionless overhead dived down head-first, holding his wings close to his body, and plummeted deep into the water. A second later the bird was on his way to a nest in a dead oak tree on the shore, a croaker in his beak. We watched a pair of black ducks to our left bobbing on the ripples like toy boats. Then suddenly one disappeared from sight, and Speck said it had plunged to the river bottom to dredge the mud with its beak in search of choice tidbits. After fully half a minute the bird reappeared, and the second duck took its turn and dived out of sight. Then our attention was diverted by a flock of barn swallows coming from the south shore. They swooped down as at a given signal, and without slackening speed, each cut the water with his beak to get a drink. Then they went up as fast as they had come down and faded into the pines on the north shore. A split second later a turtle pushed his snake-like head through the water and turned his beady eyes toward our boat. When he saw us he blinked and sank from view. This prompted Speck to explain that the turtle was highly regarded by the Algonkians, and he told us several tales that he had picked up from the Indians about turtle lore.

Suddenly it dawned on us that the study of nature is highly important and necessary for a thorough understanding of primitive living. These birds over the river, the fish beneath the surface, and the animals on its banks all played a role in the daily life of the early man who dwelt on its shores. He chose this stream as a place of abode not only because of its natural advantages, and because it was an inexhaustible source of food, but because he felt himself a part of nature's scheme, a feeling which we moderns seldom experience. As we learn to understand more about Delaware's plants, birds, and animals, we shall be better qualified to understand the primitive mind and to interpret archaeological findings.

As the afternoon wore on, we anchored in one cove after another, wading ashore to seek suitable places for former sites. We walked through old cornfields and freshly harrowed soil, our eyes turned down to the earth. Now and then one of us—for Tony and Jim were apt pupils—would pick up a potsherd, an arrowhead, a stone scraper, a battered hammerstone, or some other vestige of Indian industry. Before the day ended we had located four different sites along the river worthy of further archaeological study, and our pockets were crammed with miscellaneous specimens.

The fourth site we located was situated along a sharp vertical bank which arose fully eight feet above the water level. The field was not under cultivation and was overgrown with tall grass and weeds. The soil was visible only along the edge of the bank where the sod had washed away. On the southeastern side of the

site a little stream, called Indian Cabin Creek on the early land
patents, empties into Indian River. It was apparently named
because of an Indian settlement on its banks, although nothing
of that settlement remained above the ground. As we explored
the bank we began to pick up old shells, stone chips, and sherds
which had washed out. We walked cautiously to prevent a
cave-in because the rains and tides had undermined the bank
and its face was actually concave. Suddenly Speck left us and
scrambled down to the water's edge and began to scratch in the
bank with his penknife. Then he called up to us,

"Look what's down here."

We climbed down beside him and he held out a handful of
broken bones. They were the finger bones from a human hand,
badly decomposed. Where he had been scratching, in the face
of the bank, the darkened earth of a grave was plainly visible
against the white sand. The skeleton—for it was certain there
were more bones in the bank—was about four feet deep. It was
apparent that we needed spades, trowels, and brushes to remove
it—a full day's work. Through my mind flashed memories of two
days' digging with Dr. Stewart in Rehoboth in search of human
remains, and almost a year's toil at the Moore Shell Heap which
was also fruitless as far as human remains were concerned. Here
we were with a grave at our fingertips, and the only tool in the
party was Speck's penknife. Such are the unexpected thrills and
disappointments of seeking stone-age men. That which we had
not been hunting was now thrust upon us.

The sun had already slid down into the western pine woods,
and evening breezes were blowing in from the ocean. It would
be dark before we could sail back to Tony's place for digging
tools. To make matters worse, Speck and I were both scheduled
to start back to Wilmington the next morning and we could not
change our plans. There was nothing to do but mark the grave,
which we did, and return in the future to excavate it. Reluc-
tantly we waded out to the boat and turned her nose toward the
White House Farm as darkness closed in behind us.

There is an addendum to the foregoing episode that saddens
one to relate. At the very next opportunity we returned to Indian

River Hundred, and eagerly hastened to the burial site, burdened with compass, camera, measuring tools, and digging implements. Alas, what a disappointment. Since our previous visit the tide had completely washed away at least ten feet of the bank. The skeleton, and all the data with it, had gone to the bottom of Indian River and had been carried out to sea, probably to wash up on an isolated beach. We tested the field, but could not find anything of unusual interest, and no evidence of human burials. From all indications, the most interesting part of the site had washed away little by little each year and nothing of importance was left. Archaeology has its disappointments as well as rewards.

❊   ❊   ❊

Cedar Creek is one of many Sussex County waterways that runs westward from the watershed in the middle of the state, then straggles through woods and marshland on its way down to Delaware Bay. Tall southern white cedars, with straight and smooth trunks, used in the last century for masts and hull planks of sailing ships, grow along its quiet banks. A few miles east of Milford, Delaware, near Fort Saulsbury, the creek crosses through a large tidal marsh and empties into the bay at a little fishermen's resort called Cedar Beach.

Cedar Beach lies between Bowers Beach on the north and Slaughter Beach to the south, two of Delaware's quaint bayside fishing settlements. These resorts were largely patronized by oystermen in the 1800's, and one day of the year is still observed as a holiday, a survival of the good old days when oysters were more plentiful than now. The second Thursday in August is known in southern Delaware as "Big Thursday" and has been an institution since 1852, dating back to the time when a law prohibited tonging oysters between May 1 and August 10. The Sussex and Kent County oyster-loving farmers eagerly awaited the opening of the season and turned out with their families in covered wagons and hayracks to tong oysters and feast on them raw or roasted, amid fiddling, singing, dancing, and drinking. The subsequent postponement of the opening date of the oyster season to September 1 made little difference once the custom had been established, and the crowds still came each year on Big Thursday, as they do today, for an outing on the bayside. Black Saturday, which follows Big Thursday, was also set aside as a special day to allow the Negroes to celebrate the opening of the oyster season. The colored folks still gather at Bowers Beach on Black Saturday to have a good time. Thus a current social frolic among the whites and blacks had its origin in the oyster beds.

If it were possible to project ourselves into the past before the coming of either the whites or blacks, we should witness another oystering social frolic at Cedar Beach, and probably at Bowers Beach and Slaughter Beach, too. I will speak only of Cedar Beach, however, because there we have found tangible evidence under the sod which enables us to reconstruct partially at least the particulars of this prehistoric oyster fete.

Cedar Beach would have probably escaped archaeological scrutiny, as have the other near-by beaches, if it were not for one of the cottagers, a retired and eccentric old bachelor. He decided to build a little house along the creek and make it a permanent home instead of a mere summer shack like those occupied by his neighbors. There, secluded from the rest of the world, he sought a simple livelihood by fishing in the bay, raising a flock of chickens, and cultivating a few vegetables in the field adjacent to his house. His only winter companions were his cats, and he owned never less than a dozen at a time. These animals, all of the back-alley variety, had plenty to eat in the fish heads and tails and other scraps from their owner's table.

My good friend L. T. Alexander met the old bachelor on one of his summer fishing trips to Cedar Creek, and seeing the newly cultivated field near the house, asked if he could look for Indian stones, on the chance that he might find an arrowhead or two. Permission was readily granted, although the old fellow probably thought my friend was daft to waste time looking for common stones when the weakfish were running by the thousands in the bay. Alexander has three hobbies—photography, fishing, and archaeology—which are always competing for his leisure time. His fishing trips usually end up with the archaeology triumphant, and when we have been associated on a digging mission, he frequently wanders off to take some pictures or to throw a line in a pool that seems to hold promise.

Scarcely had Alexander stepped into the field when he found the earth littered with shells. Never before in his life had he seen a field so completely blanketed. He couldn't take more than two steps without putting his foot down on oyster shells. He saw that the shells had lost their whiteness and interior luster and had the characteristic grayness of shells that have long lain buried in the earth. He continued his walk through the field, and within a few minutes had picked up a perfect arrowhead and half a dozen broken ones as well as several potsherds.

When, upon his return to Wilmington, he related his experience we lost no time in making an excursion to Cedar Beach for the express purpose of investigating this new, unrecorded site. We were accompanied on this visit by two other members of the Archaeological Society, James Scott, who has a tireless back for wielding a spade, and the veteran collector Arch Crozier whom I have previously mentioned as one of Delaware's leading archaeological students.

We arrived at the old bachelor's bungalow early in the morning, and found him mending one of his nets on the back stoop, surrounded by cats. He recognized Alexander, and was amenable to the suggestion that we be permitted to dig some test holes in his corn field.

"I don't mind," he said, "as long as you-all fill the holes when you're done. But it sure seems like a waste of God's good time when you could be catchin' fish in the bay. They are certainly biting right smart today, too."

We promised to fill the holes when we were done, and thanked him with some cigars and a package of chewing tobacco which he accepted with great pleasure.

"Maybe the old fellow is right," Alexander said when we were out of earshot. "It's a fine day for fishing." He looked yearningly toward the bay.

"Come on," said Jim Scott, "Today we dig. Tomorrow we fish."

And he handed Alexander one of the long-handled shovels and gently pushed him into the field.

We found the site as Alexander had described it, with shells so thick that Arch Crozier said they must have rained down from heaven. The field—that is the cultivated section—was a modest plot of dry, sandy land covering only four or five acres flanked on two sides by marshes and on the third by the creek.

After several hours of excavating—employing the technique of digging exploratory test trenches—we confirmed the fact that the shells had been plowed out of pits in the earth. As at Slaughter Creek, the plow blade had knifed through the humus into the top layers of the shell pits and scattered the shells throughout the field.

Having established the origin of the shells, we next concentrated on one of the shell pits or "pockets," to use a term more descriptive of its character, to which our trench led us. The pocket was roughly circular in shape, having a diameter of four feet. It extended three feet down into the ground, slightly tapering to a saucer-shaped bottom. It was packed solidly with oyster shells and a few clams and knobbed conches, all of which we removed one by one. It was a difficult task because they were compressed so tightly together. It was necessary to work slowly so that not even the slightest clue would be overlooked.

As we neared the bottom of the pocket, we found that many of the shells showed characteristics of having once been exposed to heat. Yet they did not display the discoloration that would have resulted if they had been subjected to flame. This was, indeed, puzzling. How could the shells have been burnt but yet escaped contact with a fire? Mingled with these burnt shells were a few potsherds, flakes of brown jasper, and three jasper "turtlebacks" about four inches long none of which were burnt. These represented rejectage from arrowhead making, and as the name implies were shaped like turtles' backs. They had originally been creek pebbles, and in the stone-working process flakes had been struck off with a hammerstone, leaving the distinctively shaped core that is commonly found on southern Delaware sites.

Finally, by tedious labor, the pocket was completely cleaned of its contents and we were able to examine its interior thoroughly. The curved floor and part of the lower dirt walls were burnt a deep red—the result of exposure to intense heat. Yet there had been no charcoal or ashes among the shells, or any other indication that fire had ever been present. This was even more puzzling than the burnt shells. How, other than by fire, could the soil have been burnt?

Alexander, who had been lying on his stomach quietly studying the interior of the hole, suddenly rose to his feet.

"I give up," he said. "We find shells that are burnt but they lack marks of fire. Then we find a hole in the ground that has been singed by a fire that didn't exist. There's something queer going on."

Jim Scott eyed the huge pile of shells, and the empty hole that we were obliged to fill, and rubbed his aching back.

"You were right," he said flatly. "We should have gone fishing in the first place."

When the day ended we were no closer to solving the riddle than at the start. In fact, the problem was more complex, for we had excavated a second pocket and found it identical with the first. It, too, contained burnt shells and fire-stained walls, but completely lacked any evidence of flame or fire. The second pocket contained no potsherds or turtlebacks—only two triangular arrowpoints of brown jasper.

This trip was one of many to Cedar Beach before we were able to satisfy our curiosity. Artifacts and pottery were extremely rare, and we found no evidence of any kind in the soil of house supports, burials, fireplaces, or similar features that are usually present on the site of an aboriginal village. We were convinced that the shell pockets had existed for a useful purpose, yet we felt that they were intended for a different use from the pits at Slaughter Creek Village site which Davidson identified as refuse pits, and probably correctly.

One afternoon in the late fall we stumbled on the key to the enigma. We dug into another of the shell pockets—the tenth we had excavated since our first trip—and near the bottom we found a deposit of stones. They were of all sizes, ranging from a base-ball to boulders as large as a baby's head. As we removed these stones from the pocket, we saw that everyone showed marks of having been heated in a fire. Many of them were cracked into fragments from heat—others were stained a deep red color. Before we had finished we had removed twenty-eight stones from the single pit. That was the clue we were seeking, and was confirmed in subsequent excavations when another stone-laden pit was found. It enabled us to reconstruct what had probably happened on the site and how the pockets were used. Here is the theory that we developed.

Centuries ago the natives came to Cedar Beach to gather oysters, as they had gone to Lewes and Rehoboth. The visitors to Cedar Beach apparently did not stay for a season, but remained only for a few days at a time. Presumably their permanent homes were not far distant, perhaps a few miles up the creek where we later learned that many stone artifacts had been found. One of our future tasks is to locate the village sites, if any, on the upper stretches of Cedar Creek, and compare the cultural materials with those found on the bay-side site.

After transporting a large supply of oysters to their picnic ground, the natives were confronted with the task of preparing them for consumption, since their tastes apparently ran to both raw and cooked shell food. Naturally they had no pottery cooking vessels large enough to accommodate a haul of oysters, or any of the culinary devices that modern cooks would use. So they turned to Mother Earth for aid. They dug a hole large enough to hold as many oysters as their numbers required at one feast. To build a fire in the hole and place the oysters directly in the flame would be unwise because the meat would be scorched. Therefore they built a fire on the surface of the ground near the hole, and in the flames they placed all the stones and boulders they could collect. When these stones were thoroughly heated, they were dragged out of the fire with sticks and pushed into the bottom of the pit. The oysters were then thrown into the hole on top of the hot stones until the pit was full. Water may have been poured over the shells causing steam as it seeped down to the hot stones below. The hole was finally covered with sand, thus confining the heat to the interior of the pit. Within this modified cooking pot the bivalves simmered in their own juices as the hungry natives eagerly waited.

When the barbecue pit had done its work, the sand was brushed aside and the oysters were removed one by one, shucked and devoured. No doubt the shells were easy to open because of exposure to heat, which facilitated their consumption. The same barbecue pit may have been used several times on one outing—and probably was. Certainly the same stones were removed and used again and again, because stones are exceedingly rare in Sussex County.

After the feast was over, the barbecue holes served a secondary purpose, we speculated, as garbage containers. The waste shells were pushed into the convenient holes to fill them and also to leave the picnic ground free from some of the refuse, although many shells remained to litter the ground.

Admittedly this explanation is purely theoretical and may be disproved in future archaeological work. But it is the best we can offer to date on the basis of meager evidence. It is unquestionably a satisfactory explanation of the discolored clay walls and the burnt shells that had perplexed us. The walls had obviously been discolored by contact with the hot stones, even though no fires had ever burnt in the pits. Similarly, the shells which rested against the stones also bore the tell-tale marks of heat although they had no direct exposure to fire.

Whether our deductions are correct or not as to the specific method used in preparing the oysters, the fact remains that exploitation of the oyster beds of Delaware Bay is an old, old custom. The evidence at Lewes, Rehoboth, Slaughter Creek, and more recently at Cedar Beach proves beyond a shadow of doubt that oystering and clamming had become well established institutions on the bay long before white man set foot in the New World.

One would hesitate to say that the rural practice of visiting the bay on Big Thursday and Black Saturday is one that was indirectly borrowed from the native custom of making excursions to the coast for oysters. Nevertheless the similarity be-speaks an American heritage that cannot be overlooked by one seeking to explain the genesis of backwoods folk custom. It goes without contradiction that each generation walks in the foot-steps of its predecessors, and the well-tramped paths of the native certainly led his white successor to the food stores of the bay.

8.

Crane Hook Saga

THREE miles east of downtown Wilmington, in the heart of the city's industries, the Christina River empties into the Delaware. A low, triangular plot of land between the confluence of the two rivers has been known since the beginning of written history in Delaware as Crane Hook. The name seems to have been derived from the cranes (perhaps herons) which the early settlers observed nesting in the vicinity.

Following the settlement by the Swedes in 1638 at the "Rocks" on the Christina River, the fertile land at Crane Hook was soon laid out in farms. In 1665 a log church was built on the tract by the Swedish and Dutch congregation as their joint place of worship. Known as the Crane Hook Church, it served them for thirty-two years, and in 1699 was abandoned for the stone structure today called Old Swedes Church.

The names of the property owners living at Crane Hook were recorded as early as 1685, but it was not until March 25, 1751, that the most prominent family associated with the tract, the Aldriches, established tenure. Peter Sigfredus Aldrich was the first member of this family to live on Crane Hook, and he built a dwelling which was remodeled in 1785 by one of his sons, Lucas by name. Lucas fixed his initials under the gable on the north side of the family manse with the date of renovation. The house, with the initials and date still in plain view, is the last vestige of the colonial settlement at Crane Hook, and one marvels how it alone survived extinction as industry closed in on all sides and forced the other residents to move to less industrial neighborhoods. During the commercial expansions beginning in the last century, industrial plants began to appear at Crane Hook—the Pyrites Plants, Tannin Corporation, Lobdell Car Wheel Works, Crane Hook Oil Company, Marine Terminal, and others. Eventually nothing remained of the once extensive tract or its dwellings except the single Aldrich house and about five acres of farmland adjacent to it. Even today the house is still occupied by tenants, a proud relic of yesteryear.

In the course of digging foundations during the erection of the plants, workmen frequently encountered relics in the soil harking back to the earlier Dutch, Swedish, and English settlers. These relics comprised broken dishware, crockery, musket and cannon balls, dated coins, copper buttons, bricks, white clay pipestems, and so forth. Moreover, from slightly greater depths they unearthed stone relics that antedated the odds and ends remaining from the historic occupation. This focused archaeological attention on Crane Hook.

One of the most significant discoveries was made in 1882. Workmen digging a slip at the Lobdell Car Wheel Works on the southern bank of the Christina struck an unusual archaeological feature called a cache. At a depth of three and one-half feet from the surface of the ground they discovered more than sixty argillite blades buried in one lot, arranged together like the petals of a flower. These stones were of the type which Hilborne Cresson had called paleoliths, and the finding of sixty together caused great furore among the local followers of Dr. Abbott's theories relating to paleolithic man in the Delaware Valley. The workmen engaged in the project divided up the cache, and the blades were never again seen all together. Eleven of them eventually turned up in Peabody Museum in Boston; two went to the Museum of the American Indian in New York through the local barber collector, Fred Hilbiber; two reached Joseph Wigglesworth; three found their way to Arch Crozier's collection, but the others vanished into thin air. In a short time they were forgotten. Many years later we began to compile data on Delaware caches, and the Lobdell cache again came to light. In 1940, hopeful of obtaining some possible shreds of information, Arch Crozier and I visited the late George Lobdell, Jr., who had suc-

ceeded his father as principal owner of the company. Mr. Lobdell, who had then passed his ninetieth birthday, was feeble, but
his memory was clear. He sat at the old rolltop oak desk in the
same office his father had occupied, and, despite his advanced
years, came to work every day and directed the activities of the
company. He seemed like a character from a Galsworthy novel
as he arose to greet us, stroking his long gray beard. In faltering
words he told us how the cache had been found, and went on
to say that from time to time other stone articles had been dug
up on the property. Then he personally escorted us through the
yards to the river bank where the argillite blades had come to
light more than fifty years before. When we returned to the
office, pausing once or twice on the way back for the old gentleman to catch his breath, he asked if we cared to see some of
the mineral specimens he had collected in his younger days
while on a tour in the West. Crozier, who is also a student of
minerals, shells, birds and other natural things, as well as Indian
lore, jumped at the opportunity and I tagged along.

The old gentleman pointed out a wooden staircase leading to
the unoccupied second floor of the old office building, but he
remained behind after excusing himself with polite dignity. We
learned later that because of his infirmity he had not climbed
these stairs in many years. The steps creaked as we ascended
to a dark upstairs hall. Along the wall was a cupboard reaching
almost to the ceiling. Behind its fogged glass doors were specimens of quartz, crystals, obsidian, iron, copper, petrified wood,
and other minerals mostly of commercial value. The hinges on
the doors squeaked as we opened them for the first time in
twenty years. Crozier, with the typical appraising touch of a
collector, examined each object carefully. Then he reached into
one of the darkest corners of the cupboard and removed a dusty
stone of different shape than the other specimens. "It looks like
one of the argillite cache blades," he exclaimed, handing it to
me for inspection.

Again he reached into the inner depths of the cupboard and
brought out two more blades identical with the first. "This is as
much fun as digging them up from the ground," he said, as his

head and shoulders again disappeared into the cupboard. This time, to my astonishment, he brought out three more of the blades. Before we closed the cupboard doors he had found nine argillite blades, each approximately the size of a human hand and alike as peas in a pod.

We hurried downstairs and showed them to Mr. Lobdell.

When the old gentleman saw the blades his eyes grew bright and he smiled. He recalled that he had salvaged these nine from the original cache of sixty, but had long since forgotten about them. At our suggestion, he generously presented them to the Archaeological Society of Delaware, and they may now be seen in the museum.

There seems little doubt today that the cache represented, not paleoliths, but quarry blades obtained at an argillite outcropping either in New Jersey or Pennsylvania. There are no argillite veins in Delaware. The natives quarried huge chunks of the stone by breaking it loose from the vein with stone mauls and heavy sticks. Then they reduced the chunks to suitable blades, oval in shape, which could in turn be converted into arrowheads, knives, spearpoints, and other chipped implements. These blades were then carried back with them to their homes and camps to be fabricated as needed. Before chipping quarried materials it was a common aboriginal practice to bury the stone in the earth, under the assumption that the moisture of the soil "freshened" the stone and made it easier to flake with a bone tool. Caches of similar quarry blades have been reported from all parts of the United States and, in fact, another cache of argillite blades was excavated some years ago near Claymont. The stones in the second cache were also neatly arranged in a daisy-petal pattern.

When the Crane Hook cache was originally found, and other relics uncovered in the course of industrial expansion, many Wilmington Indian relic collectors were attracted to the area. Some of the neighboring fields were still in farmland and many artifacts were turned up during the spring plowing. This site was one of Joe Wigglesworth's favorite haunts, and Arch Crozier's earliest surface hunting was done in these fields. Both men amassed sizable collections at Crane Hook, Crozier's alone consisting of several thousand specimens which he has carefully catalogued. The material he gathered includes arrowheads, spearheads, and knives of a wide variety of stones of many hues. The stemmed arrowpoints dominate the collection since only about fifteen percent are of the triangular variety so common in southern Delaware. Crozier's Crane Hook material also includes scraping and cutting tools of stone many fashioned from broken arrowheads which had been salvaged and reworked by the stone-age artisan to make them serviceable for other purposes. Grooved stone axes, celts, pitted hammerstones, small pestles, and abrading stones are well represented. Gorgets with from two to five holes, pendants and bannerstones are both present.* The clay potsherds he gathered consisted of relatively few unrelated fragments, a contrast to the numerous sherds gathered from south Delaware sites. He also found a few pieces of a soapstone pot, a soft gray stone which the natives used in making cooking vessels, pipes, and ceremonial objects.

Soapstone—or steatite to use its proper name—was used in varying amounts by the natives of Delaware. Especially on the presumable village sites along the Murderkill and St. Jones Creeks (which have not yet been excavated) many fragments of soapstone cooking vessels can be found on the surface of the ground. Judging by these fragments, the vessels were oval in shape and had lugs on each end which served as handles. There are no natural deposits of this stone in Delaware the nearest vein crosses at Christina, Pennsylvania, a small town near the Gap. Here, many years ago, along Williams Branch of Octararo Creek, Harry Wilson, a mineralogist of West Chester, Pa , located an aboriginal soapstone quarry. Those of us who have visited this quarry site have found stone picks and chisels which the natives used to dig out the soft soapstone, and many portions of incomplete soapstone vessels.* We believe that some of the prehistoric natives of Delaware visited this quarry to obtain the precious soapstone that is found today in scattered fragments on local sites. The early colonists also used soapstone, which retains heat longer than ordinary stones, on which to bake

* (For a description of these various artifacts, see Chapter 9.)

bread and cake. Today soapstone is used commercially as a source of talc—another raw product whose use dates back to America's prehistoric past.

The members * of the Archaeological Society of Delaware turned their attention to Crane Hook on Saturday, May 13, 1939, hopeful of digging up information before the last remnant of the site was completely destroyed.

The little knoll on which the excavators worked had formerly been the ascending bank of the Delaware River, although the water had receded years ago leaving a marsh three-quarters of a mile wide between the old bank and the present river shore. The hill rose to a maximum height of twenty-five feet above mean Delaware River level and covered four to five acres. A north-south trench was first dug on the western slope of the hill. This trench was four feet wide, four feet deep, and fifty feet long. The area to be excavated, west of the trench, was staked out in five-foot squares, and each stake was numbered and the base line tied in to permanent bench marks. Each excavator was assigned one of the five-foot squares, and he stood in the trench and worked against the vertical western wall in his section, shaving away the earth with his trowel. As the artifacts were uncovered, they were catalogued by number, measured according to depth and triangulated to the two nearest stakes before they were removed from the soil. This permitted a blueprint to be made showing exactly where anything of interest was found. Many photographs, both still and motion pictures were made, and a complete series of notes and measurements were recorded for future reference.

For ten months, on Saturdays, Sundays, holidays, and in the evenings, the trench was widened, and eventually had been moved a considerable distance up the slope. The original intent was to advance the trench across the entire knoll, maintaining its fifty-foot width all the way, thus bisecting the site. But our

* Those participating in the work were Arch Crozier, James Scott, Arthur Volkman, Seal Brooks, Geiger Omwake, Theodore Buckalew, Arthur Kamperman, Ella McComb, C. V. Davis, S. C. Robinson, L. T. Alexander, Stanley Swiento-chowski, John Swientochowski and myself.

Uncovering three objects at Crane Hook: a gorget (white object in center background); stone axe (beside trowel handle); and clay pipe (at point of trowel).

Indians making a log dugout. The native on the right burns away the log, while the workman on the left chops at the charred fragments with a stone maul and a celt.

plans had to be changed, for during the course of the work the property was leased as a plant site, and workmen were soon busy digging foundations for the buildings to be erected. This impending doom necessitated faster work on the part of the excavators, so a smaller test trench, five feet wide, was extended all the way up the slope and across the brow of the hill from the major digging. Later the northern and southern slopes were intensively test-pitted. Finally, with the assistance of workmen from the Wilimington Marine Terminal, the topsoil was removed from the northern slope of the site and carefully sieved through a screen. The exposed subsoil was then examined horizontally for postmolds or other possible disturbances. In the meantime the workers engaged on the industrial plant began completely to level off the hillock, and during their work a deep vertical face was maintained which allowed an examination of the soil in a profile twenty-five feet deep.

Almost all traces of the early Indian occupation were concentrated in the humus layer, which varied in depth from eight inches to fourteen inches. The upper seven inches of this humus, the plow zone, had been cultivated since colonial days, and as a result its contents were badly disturbed and jumbled. Throughout the humus we uncovered refuse left there by the Dutch and Swedish settlers; hand-wrought iron nails and spikes, lead musket balls, white clay pipestems, gun flints, a large penny, fragments of gravestone, a copper plate engraved with a name, a fragment of whetstone for sharpening plows, and other miscellanous and intrinsically worthless objects. Yet they clearly revealed how each generation leaves behind in the soil traces of its passing, the theory enunciated by Thomsen in 1830 and now a fundamental principle in archaeological research.

The humus also produced a large variety of artifacts and stone refuse remaining from aboriginal implement-making. Bushels of fractured and flaked quartz and quartzite pebbles and chips were removed, illustrating how extensive was the stone-working industry on the site. During the sieving operation previously mentioned, at least five wheelbarrows full of stone rejectage were hauled away. Although quartz, quartzite, and jasper predominated, argillite, rhyolite, and other exotic stones were present. These had unquestionably been imported from the nearest quarries as blanks, and tools were fabricated by artisans on the site. The artifacts that were uncovered consisted of the identical types of utensils and implements that Crozier and others had found on the surface during successive plowing year after year. In view of the frequent visitations to the site by collectors, it was surprising that many relics remained, yet we catalogued more than two hundred arrowheads, ten hammerstones, eighty-six scraping tools, eight stone knives, five axes, two celts, two bannerstones, three stone drills, two clay pipestems of aboriginal design, and several hundred potsherds. The sherds were all tiny, none larger than a few inches square, probably representing not more than eight or ten different vessels. Very little relative to the size of the pots could be established from the unrelated fragments, but several sherds from the bottoms indicated that the pots were pointed, typical of the woodland varieties. The pottery was meager when compared to the abundance of sherds found in the Sussex County excavations. Bone refuse and bone and shell artifacts were completely absent.

Despite diligent search no definite aboriginal house supports could be found in the soil, nor the slightest indication of any Indian graves.

One disturbance extending seven inches into the subsoil was a shallow, saucer-shaped depression two feet in diameter. It contained a mass of fire-cracked stones and had apparently served the natives as a hearth or fire pit. The top had been torn loose by the plow. It contained only three burnt potsherds and bits of charcoal. Many other fire-cracked stones scattered through the humus suggested the former presence of other equally shallow firepits which the plow had obliterated.

John Swientochowski and his brother Stanley encountered the most interesting aboriginal feature of the entire excavation in their section. It was a pit, or trench, that extended down into the subsoil from the humus, whose exact purpose could not be established. It contained black earth remaining from decayed

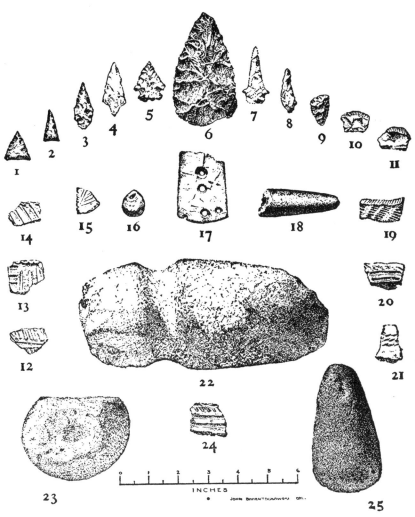

A few of the artifacts excavated at the Crane Hook Site. Nos. 1 to 11 are stone points and scrapers. Nos. 12, 13, 14, 19, 20, 21, 24 are tiny pot fragments. No. 17 is a gorget; 18 a pipe stem; 22 a grooved stone axe; 23 a hammerstone; 25 a celt

organic matter, charcoal, and, in association, a large grooved axe in perfect condition weighing about five pounds, a stone gorget containing five holes, the stem of an aboriginal clay pipe, and a fragmentary spearhead.

Beneath the humus of the site was a hard, yellowish clay subsoil and sand, the Cape May formation which, as we have remarked, was deposited in the last interglacial stage. Nowhere was there a single clue to man or animal in this older deposit, no artifacts, no disturbances. Moreover, because of the work of the industrial crews with their mechanical digging tools, we were able to inspect this subsoil very carefully over the entire site to a greater depth than otherwise would have been possible.

After the site had been thoroughly excavated and all the data weighed, we were forced to conclude that the occupational layer had been very shallow. The paucity of pits and fireplaces; the absence of Indian graves; the scarcity of pottery and agricultural utensils (stone hoes, mortars, etc.); the absence of bone refuse, shell refuse, carbonized corn and beans, convinced us that it could not have been a permanent village site in our conception of the term.

We concluded that Crane Hook was probably a large hunting and fishing camp occupied only at certain times of the year by natives who came from some other not far distant villages. During the time the site was occupied, agriculture was probably not practised; pottery was used only to a limited extent; but hunting accessories, such as arrowheads, stone knives, scrapers, and other stone artifacts were made in abundance and used extensively. Because of the absence of white-manufactured commodities in the lower part of the humus, we assumed that the site had been in existence prehistorically, that is to say, prior to 1600. There are no references to Indians having occupied the site in any of the early narratives or on any of the old maps. Where did the Crane Hook folk come from? There is no certain way of knowing, but their permanent home may have been a village within the limits of Wilmington which was destroyed when the city was built. Or they may have come from villages

situated elsewhere on the Delaware River, presumably above
Wilmington.

* * *

The most exciting phase of the entire excavation at Crane
Hook, while falling under the scope of archaeology, was not of
aboriginal origin. Yet it was a lesson in how the earth retains
the story of the past. When the working trench was dug we
purposely avoided a small clump of trees on the edge of the knoll
because it was reported traditionally that a white man had been
buried there. Since we were seeking older remains we saw no
need to disturb more recent graves. Consequently we dug outside of the trees, cautioning our excavators to avoid trespassing
on the plot. As the laborers began to excavate for the industrial
plant, however, these trees were chopped down and the earth
removed. We warned the foreman to be on the alert for a human
skeleton so that it could be properly removed and reburied.

One evening the foreman phoned me at my home.

"Can you come down to Crane Hook?" he said. "My workmen
have found a skeleton." I got in my car early the next morning
and drove to the site.

The foreman showed me a skull and some leg and arm bones
which had been dislodged from the bank. He had exercised
good judgment by stopping the laborers and moving them to
another section when the bones were encountered. I completed
the removal of the remains, which proved to be those of a white
male of middle age. The bones were taken to the Marine
Terminal office to be reburied.

Several days later the foreman phoned again and said that his
men had encountered loose black dirt that resembled the first
grave. Although no bones had been exposed, he said he was
certain that there was another skeleton in the bank. His hunch
was well founded. In fact, before the work had ended, *twelve*
different graves were encountered in the earth where the clump
of trees had stood. There was always the possibility that Indian
skeletons might be found, and consequently each grave was

carefully uncovered, using the approved techniques that have already been described. This gave some of the members of the Archaeological Society valuable experience in removing human remains from the soil, even though all the skeletons turned out to be those of white persons.

In all the graves, badly disintegrated hand-wrought coffin nails of the colonial period were present. Nothing else remained of the wooden coffins. Several round-headed pins that had fastened the shrouds were also found, and these were of a type outmoded in Delaware about 1830. This was an important clue in helping us date the graves. Two of the male skeletons had copper buttons near the bones of their wrists and knees. There was no doubt that these buttons had formerly been attached to the coat sleeves and knee breeches of the deceased. The latter type of garment must be dated earlier than 1800, for after that date the long trousers became popular in men's styles. The copper salts from the buttons had acted as a preservative, and shreds of cloth and thread were still clinging to the buttons. The remainder of the garments which the corpses had worn had, of course, decayed from exposure to the moist earth.

The skeletons were all buried on their backs, legs extended and arms at the sides, usually with the hands crossed over the abdomen.

One of the bodies was buried in a clay-brick vault built beneath the ground, a mortuary custom that is now obsolete but apparently was once widely used in early Delaware, especially for prominent persons. This vault had been built three feet below the surface of the earth. It was not of the more recent type of vault countersunk in the ground with the lid even with the surface. The vault was oblong in shape, consisting of four brick walls. The two side walls were seven and one-half feet long. The end wall at the head was two feet in width and the end wall at the feet was one foot, eight inches, in width, showing that the structure had slightly tapered from head to foot. The individual bricks were eight inches by four inches by two and a half inches, and were imperfectly shaped and were of the baked clay variety made in the 1700's.

The remains—a female aged thirty to forty years—had been placed in a wooden casket, laid to rest in the earth, and walled around on four sides with the bricks. Wooden planks had then been laid over the top of the brick walls to serve as a cover for the vault. There were no bricks across the top or bottom—in fact the bottom consisted only of the hard clay floor.

There were no grave stones or markers for this burial or any of the others, and the question of the specific dates of the graves was difficult to ascertain.

Later, as we began to question various persons about this unrecorded cemetery, we learned that there had formerly been a gravestone in the clump of trees, but it had been broken by vandals, and one of the executives of the Marine Terminal had taken it to his office for safe keeping. We inspected the broken stone, which was inscribed with an epitaph reading as follows:

In
Memory of
Samuel Watson
who departed this life
December 16
1813 aged
32 years

None of the remaining eleven graves had been marked with stones, and naturally we combed all the records available in an effort to identify Samuel Watson in the hope that we might find clues that held the identity of the other bodies. We were fortunately able to establish, with the coöperation of Miss Jeanette Eckman and Jeremiah Sweeney, two students of Delaware history, that in 1813 when Samuel Watson was buried, the tract of land was under the point lien of Peter Sigfredus Aldrich and Samuel Aldrich. They had inherited the land in 1806 from their father, Lucas Aldrich, and it was in the possession of the sons until 1818.

All facts considered, it seemed reasonable to conclude that the burial plot, within a stone's throw of the old Aldrich house, was a private graveyard for members of that family and probably was used as far back as 1751. The graves may originally have been marked with wooden crosses or some other perishable materials which decayed with the passing of the years, and eventually the graveyard was completely forgotten. All of the bones we excavated were transported to the Marine Terminal to be reburied in a common grave suitably marked with a stone plaque.

One can easily become a sentimentalist as he reflects on the destruction of the Crane Hook site to make way for modern commercial developments. As we laid bare the colonial graves and the stones artifacts of an earlier era, blue-shirted workmen swinging their dinner pails came to their jobs in the morning and hurried home at night, uninterested in a dead past. Tramp steamers turned into the Christina River with whistles shrieking; and freight trains rumbled past, spewing smoke and cinders over the bones we were uncovering. A few feet away, a noisy steam shovel gutted the earth we had so patiently troweled inch by inch.

Today the site we excavated is completely covered by new factory buildings. Beneath their foundations and under the newly laid railroad tracks many old secrets still lie sleeping, unaffected by the throb of industry. The Indian civilization and the settlement of Swedish, Dutch, and English farmers which supplanted it are no longer remembered. It seems inevitable that the present industrial complexion of Crane Hook will be altered by generations to come. Walls will crumble, roofs will fall, and men will indifferently walk, as they do today, on the ruins of the past that Mother Earth never forgets.

*　　*　　*

After the excavation at Crane Hook had been completed and a report of the results published, members of the Archaeological Society decided to investigate another New Castle County site to determine how it compared with Crane Hook. The site that was selected lay several miles north of Crane Hook, near Claymont, at the junction of Naaman's Creek with the Delaware

River. It was only a short distance from the site of Cresson's pile structure long since disappeared, and was on the southern bank of the creek on property owned by the Worth Steel Company. Permission was obtained from Mr. E. H. Worth to conduct a small test digging. A committee consisting of H. G. Omwake, William Habbart, James Scott, Arch Crozier, John Swientochowski, and myself were assigned to make the investigation.

The site, like the one at Crane Hook, was along the Delaware River bank, high enough to protect the occupants against the rising tides. It, too, was in the heart of an industrial section, and had been partially destroyed by railroad tracks and plants. A residue of oil, carried down the river from the Marcus Hook refineries, fouled its banks, and clouds of thick smoke hung over the area. The site had formerly been in farmland, and when under cultivation it was one of the favorite hunting grounds of Claymont relic seekers. Both Arch Crozier and William Habbart had gathered large collections from the site in bygone years. The material, which was carefully inspected before we began digging, was identical with the stone artifacts found at Crane Hook.

There was no intention to launch an extensive excavation unless the preliminary tests revealed conclusive evidence of a former village with the deep black soil resulting from decayed organic matter which usually marks the sub-surface remains of a village. Above all, we wanted to gather together whatever shreds of information we could before the site was completely covered by industry. To evaluate the site, a test block approximately thirty feet square was excavated in the center of the field where most of the artifacts had been found. Then several exploratory trenches were made, running on four sides of the test. This work was done over five consecutive week-ends, for all of us were regularly employed elsewhere and could only spare Saturdays and Sundays from our salaried jobs. As at Crane Hook, large quantities of stone rejectage, fractured pebbles, fire-cracked stones, chips, and flakes were uncovered in the test trenches. A few miscellanous and unimportant arrowheads, scrapers, and tiny potsherds were unearthed. No fireplaces, pits, graves, or house foundations were found beneath the humus. In fact the humus, lacking the blackness we sought, was only a few inches thick and overlay hard, sterile clay. The plow in former years had mutilated this shallow occupied layer, and it seemed obvious that an excavating project would not justify the time and effort since the site had been so seriously disturbed. Moreover, our tests and a study of the surface and excavated specimens indicated that the site was similar to Crane Hook in that it did not house a true aboriginal village, but was only a camping place presumably occupied for a short period. Unquestionably it had been frequented by people who were culturally related to those who had camped elsewhere in northern Delaware, for example, at the little stations at Newport, Folly Woods, and Stanton. This was readily corroborated by comparing the artifacts from these locations.

It is not unlikely that the town of Claymont is built on the site of a true native village, just as many other Delaware towns sprang up where the prehistoric people had lived or camped. Possibly the river-bank site was one of their camps, of lesser size than the village. To find the true village remains would involve excavating beneath the streets and houses of the town, a project of such magnitude as to be prohibitive. Donald Cadzow, the Pennsylvania archaeologist, experienced a parallel problem during an archaeological study, and he excavated aboriginal graves and village remains beneath the pavements and houses in Washington Borough, Lancaster County, the site of a former native village or fort.

The river-bank people at Claymont may also have been itinerant hunters from one of the other native settlements which, before the coming of the whites, were located along the western shore of the Delaware at Chester, Marcus Hook, Philadelphia, Wilmington, and New Castle. Some of these settlements were permanent, while others were of a temporary nature. Unfortunately their exact identities cannot be established, because some modern cities and towns came into being before interest in archaeology had awakened. Nevertheless the story is still there in the soil covered by tons of steel and cement.

The archaeologist working in America, particularly in the heavily populated East, constantly competes with the advances of civilization which are slowly but surely encroaching upon the former occupational sites. The archaeologist also meets rivals in adverse weather conditions and high tides which often seem to be conspiring together in blotting out the story of the past. He is sometimes vexed by uncoöperative property owners and by vandals who ruin archaeological features by digging hit-or-miss solely out of curiosity or for monetary gain. We have already witnessed instances of such interference in Delaware. Frequently the archaeologist is hampered through lack of funds to enable him to pursue his work properly, although interested donors are becoming more conscious of the value of such work.

Some of the episodes related in this chapter seem to have a negative tone and may appear incomplete to the reader, especially from the standpoint of obtaining conclusive scientific data. But who knows? Issues which now seem hopelessly clouded may be clarified by future discoveries. The archaeologist's guiding philosophy is to pursue his objective religiously, gathering data where and how he can, and noting all details that are worthy of record, even though they may appear insignificant, incomplete, or even negative. As time goes on others will join in this strangest of all man-hunts, and some day the work now being done may be helpful in forging one of the links in the chain of man's knowledge of the world where he lives.

9.

Relics From the Past

THE earth where I walked that August morning was cool and soft like moss that grows in shady places. The tall cornstalks brushing my shoulders shaded the ground and kept it moist and sweet smelling. A scattering of pale quartz flakes, none larger than my little fingernail, were the clues I had been seeking between the rows of corn. For here, in this field along the banks of the Christina River, a Lenape arrowhead maker once sat cross-legged on the ground. His hammerstone bit into the pebble he held, throwing off the distinctive flakes that had marked his trade down through the years.

There on the ground where I imagined he had been sitting something sparkled in the sun. It was an arrowhead, so white that at first I thought a heart-shaped blossom had fallen in the furrow, so clear-cut that it might have been made an hour before. The rain had washed it clean, and it lay there like a jewel on a bed of velvet. I picked it up and held it to the sun. It was crystal-clear at the point, its clearness melting into a milky whiteness at the barbs and stem. No song or poem tells a story more romantic than can be read into this arrowhead. The arrowhead maker and his people are no more, but their creations in stone last for all time. There are few joys to compare with finding and preserving this tiny part of the dead centuries. For generations it lay lost and unnoticed, and then it fell my fortune to recover it.

That arrowhead I found that summer day—my first in Delaware—unlocked the door of the past for me, and I urge the young reader to seek the enjoyment of hunting arrowheads as a hobby, carefully preserving and cataloguing any specimens he finds. By heeding Joe Wigglesworth's advice previously given, the lessons of surface hunting, with its pleasures and rewards, may be readily learned. Many of the nation's foremost anthropologists began as humble amateurs, their interest in ancient cultures dating from the stone arrowheads found in boyhood. Although arrowheads are the best known, many other types of artifacts may be found in Delaware. In previous chapters reference has been made to other forms of stone and clay handiwork, but a complete classification has not been given, nor, in fact, has it ever been presented as a guide to the amateur. The following listing may, therefore, prove valuable in acquainting the amateur with the wide range of relics he can find, and will also serve as glossary for those with archaeological training. Some repetition will occur, especially as relating to specimens previously introduced in the story, but this is necessary to make the listing complete. The reader should remember that only the permanent materials have survived. The natives also made and used objects of wood, bark, skin, grass, and other perishable materials which should not be overlooked in reconstructing a story of Delaware's yesterday.

ARROWHEADS, SPEARHEADS AND KNIVES

Stone arrowpoints have been found by the thousands in Delaware fields. A common error is to call all chipped flints arrowheads, but at this late date we cannot be certain of the use for which such specimens were originally intended. Stone points were also fastened to wood, bone, and horn handles for use as knives, scrapers, perforators, and daggers as well as arrow shafts. These points were all approximately of like shape, and it is frequently difficult to distinguish between them. An object called an arrowhead may have been used as a cutting tool instead of a tip for an arrowshaft. I prefer to combine arrowheads, spearheads, and knives, calling them "stone points," without attempting to differentiate between them.

The stone points found in Delaware are fashioned from a number of types of stones, and summarized below are the most common ones as identified by Dr. Horace Richards. One cannot learn to identify these stones by reading this text, but he must see the materials in order to familiarize himself with their appearance.

STONES OBTAINED LOCALLY FROM DELAWARE PEBBLES

Quartz—a hard stone, usually white or colorless. Sometimes called white flint. When it occurs in a reddish color, it is known as *rose quartz*. Another form is *smoky quartz*, cloudy in color. *Quartz crystal*, so called, is like glass in appearance.

Quartzite—a type of sandstone occurring in various colors. Browns, red, and pinks dominate in Delaware.

Flint—(crypto-crystalline quartz) black in color.

Chert—(crypto-crystalline quartz) gray, green, creamy in color.

Jasper—(crypto-crystalline quartz) red or brown in color.

Chalcedony—(crypto-crystalline quartz) translucent, especially on the edges.

(Crypto-crystalline is a technical term used to describe the above stones which are all similar in structure but differ in color. All of these are actually forms of quartz.)

None of the above materials occur in mass in Delaware. They are all found in pebbles taken from creek and river bottoms and other sand and pebble deposits. Only one type of stone in Delaware suitable for making stone points and existing in mass (not pebbles) has been identified. This mineral has a heavy iron content, and since it is believed (not yet proved) to have been quarried by the Indians in the vicinity of Iron Hill near Newark, it is locally known as Newark Jasper.

There are other stone materials, not indigenous to the state, and yet stone points made of them are often found. This indicates that the aborigines imported stone from outside sources. Some of these are listed below.

STONES IMPORTED INTO DELAWARE FOR USE IN MAKING
STONE POINTS

Shale—grayish or brownish material which is really consolidated mud. Disintegrates very easily when exposed to weathering. Can be nicked with the fingernail.

Argillite—a more durable form of shale, although similar in appearance. Is grayish or reddish in color, and usually has a dull, weathered surface.

Rhyolite—a light-colored mineral related to granite and consisting of a mixture of feldspar and quartz. Originates in quarries on South Mountain near Gettysburg, Pennsylvania.

Flint Ridge Flint—smooth, waxen-surfaced stone usually pink in color which was mined by the natives in quarries in Ohio. Can be readily recognized by its beautiful texture. (Only a few points of Flint ridge flint have been found in Delaware.)

Pennsylvania Jasper—smooth, waxen-surfaced stone, usually chocolate brown in color. Originated at extensive aboriginal quarries near Vera Cruz, Pennsylvania.

Cohansey Quartzite—a distinctive blue-gray quartzite, found to date in pebbles along Cohansey Creek in New Jersey. A few arrowheads of this stone have been found in Delaware.

The stone points vary in size from approximately one-half inch in length to larger and more rare specimens eight or ten inches long. The points are of diverse shapes and the significance of these shapes is a subject for further study. The type of point with the bifurcated (notched) base and serrated (saw-tooth) edges is perhaps the most intriguing. The tiny bird point so common in the west is not found in Delaware. Speaking in a very broad way, there are two styles of Delaware points: the stemmed point and the unstemmed, or triangular point.

The stemmed point is shouldered to permit its being securely tied to a shaft or handle. The triangular point is often called a war point but there is every indication that it was used for the same purpose as the stemmed point. Delaware triangular points, of which large quantities are found, are most frequently broad-based, equilateral triangles, unlike the isoceles points common to Iroquoian peoples. Arrowpoints, according to the early writers, were fastened to shafts either with thongs or with glue made from fish or deer hooves.

ANTLER TINE ARROWPOINTS

Arrowpoints made of the tip or tine of a deer antler have not been found in any quantity in Delaware. The few specimens noted have been excavated in Sussex County. It is assumed that antler tine and bone were widely used by the Indians of the southern extremity of the peninsula where stone is very scarce. Captain John Smith in his *History of Virginia* speaks of the Indians on the Eastern Shore spearing fishes with spears tipped with bone.

ARROWSHAFT RUBBERS OR STRAIGHTENERS

One of the Indian's abrading tools was a stone, grooved with one or more furrows, each approximately the diameter of an arrowshaft. It is thought that the arrowshaft was worked back and forth in the groove to polish it and remove any irregularities. Arrowshaft rubbers, also called smoothers and straighteners, are generally made of abrasive stone, but several of steatite have been found.

AWLS, BONE

Bone awls are not common in Delaware; in fact, all bone artifacts are scarce. The awl is generally made of a deer or turkey bone, worked to a point by rubbing it with an abrasive stone. This rubbing gives it a smooth surface called a polish. When archaeologists speak of polished bone they refer to a fragment of bone which has been subject to workmanship for the purpose of making an artifact.

Possibly one of the major uses for the bone awl was in perforating skin or bark. It doubtless served other miscellaneous uses as a piercing tool. Frequently the joint on the bone (knuckle) was used as a natural handle for the awl.

AXES, GROOVED

The stone axe, with an encircling groove to permit fastening it to a handle, is found throughout Delaware. Axes vary in size from specimens as small as six inches long to massive types a foot or more in length. Axes were frequently manufactured from water-worn pebbles, although granitic rocks were usually preferred.

The usual form of axe is wedge-shaped, with a cutting edge on one end and a blunt edge or poll on the opposite end. The groove in Delaware axes parallels the edge of the implement. Diagonal and double-grooved axes are scarcely ever found. Specimens vary in weight from eight ounces to ten pounds.

The grooved axe is often called a tomahawk, but it is the consensus of opinion that this object was used extensively as a domestic tool and not as a weapon. Early writers tell us that when an Indian felled a tree he first used fire and then knocked away the charred portions with his stone axe. He made his log dugout in a similar way. It was necessary that he use fire inasmuch as the blade of his axe was not sharp enough to cut wood as do our modern steel tools.

BALLS

Stone balls as small as marbles and as large as baseballs have been found in Delaware. These have been pecked into shape with a hammerstone and occasionally polished. They may have been used as gaming stones. Some students call these objects bola stones, but it is not certain that the bola was used by the inhabitants of the peninsula.

BANNERSTONES

The term "bannerstone" is applied to perforated stone objects some of which are wing-shaped, suggestive of a large butterfly.

This form is known popularly as the butterfly bannerstone, although there are other specimens which do not have wings. The significance of the several shapes still remains unexplained. The central perforation extending through the middle of the bannerstone suggests that it was mounted on a staff. The bannerstone's use remains problematical, and there is no agreement as to its original purpose since it was apparently not described by any of the explorers or settlers. Recent work in the Southwest has indicated that some bannerstones were used as balancing weights on *atlatls* (spear throwers). We have not yet established that the *atlatl*, which preceded the bow and arrow as a weapon, was ever used in Delaware.

Delaware bannerstones are usually made of steatite or slate. Reworked portions of bannerstones are frequently found, indicating that the object had accidently broken in use and the pieces salvaged. The fragments were often redrilled, grooved, or otherwise refashioned for use as an ornament. Sometimes mending holes were drilled in the two halves to permit their being repaired by lacing them together with a leather thong.

The bannerstone is considered a choice item by collectors, and consequently is one of the best sought of all Indian artifacts.

BEADS

Beads are not common in Delaware, but there is record of beads of both stone and shell. Mention has been made in an earlier chapter of a mussel-shell bead found near Claymont, now on display at Peabody Museum and of the copper beads found by Leidy and Jordan. The Smithsonian Institution also has in its possession a string of shell beads found near Claymont which was presented by Hilborne Cresson. Harold T. Purnell, a private collector, owns three small shell beads found on the surface of a site near Georgetown, Delaware. Archibald Crozier owns a tiny perforated shell fragment, possibly a bead, found at Crane Hook. There is as yet no record in Delaware of glass trade beads of the contact period. Tubular bone beads are also rare in the state.

BIRDSTONES

Like the bannerstone, the birdstone is also a problematical object, undoubtedly used for ceremonial purposes. It has a bar-like body with an expanded and upward flare of either end, giving it the appearance of having a head and tail, not unlike a bird, as its name indicates. Its base is usually perforated with two holes, suggesting that it was probably laced with a thong, perhaps as a personal adornment or as a canoe ornament. Birdstones are exceptionally rare in Delaware, and the few specimens that have been recorded are very crude when compared to beautiful specimens found elsewhere in the United States.

BLADES

The term "blade," as used locally, serves to describe the flat, generally oval-shaped pieces of stone which have been flaked to shape. Those bearing secondary chipping along their edges may have been used as knives. The term "quarry blade" describes the flat blades, worked out at a stone quarry from a larger mass, which are not usually retouched along the edges. The blades were then transported to a suitable place for fabrication into implements. Quarry blades of jasper and rhyolite, as well as argillite, have been found in Delaware.

BODKIN

The bodkin is a flat needle, ranging from six to ten inches in length, made of highly-polished bone, usually from a sliver of an animal's rib. It is generally perforated with one hole. The supposition is that the bodkin was used as a needle in making nets. Bodkins, to date, have been found only in Sussex County, and all have been excavated. There is no record of surface specimens.

CANOES '

A canoe would not ordinarily be classed as an archaeological specimen, at least in the East where wooden objects are seldom found during excavations of ancient sites. In 1933, however, a log dugout was unearthed in Delaware, which necessitates classing it with other known artifacts. During the deepening and widening of Pepper's Creek, a tributary of Indian River, the canoe was found near Dagworthy Landing. It was buried in a bed of sand about six feet deep which apparently had been responsible for its preservation. Made of a pine log, with the marks of crude tools still visible, it is twelve feet long, eighteen inches wide, and twelve inches deep. At this writing the canoe is in the possession of the Steen family of Dagsboro. Its age is unknown, but is undoubtedly of the aboriginal type. Unfortunately it was not removed scientifically and consequently no accurate data are available regarding the soil stratum in which it lay.

CELTS'

Celts are often referred to as ungrooved stone axes. The celt is a wedge-shaped implement with one blunt end and another end sharpened to a cutting edge. Some celts may have been used in the hand, striking the blunt end with a hammerstone, just as a modern chisel is employed. Other celts were hafted to wood handles and were used as weapons or domestic axes. Sometimes celts are known to amateur students as skinning knives, although it is questionable that they were made primarily for this purpose.

Small celts made from creek pebbles are found more frequently in Delaware than the larger specimens so common on Iroquois sites. The celt in Delaware, however, in any of its forms is not common and was apparently not as widely used as the grooved axe.

DISCOIDALS '

The true polished discoidal found so abundantly in the Midwest is totally absent in Delaware. Stones of discoidal shape five or six inches in diameter have been found, but these may have been hammerstones or mullers, or perhaps gaming pieces. The perforated discoidal has not yet been recorded in Delaware.

DRILLS

For perforating woods, shell, bone, dried clay, and stone, the Indian employed a drill made of a hard stone. In appearance a stone drill resembles an arrowhead with an elongated point. It was fastened to the shaft and revolved by spinning in the bow string. The backward and forward motion of the drill served to perforate the surface to be drilled. Some drills appear not to have been hafted and may have been used in the hand as an augur or boring tool.

FLAKE KNIVES

To convert a flake into a knife of great utility, the aboriginal craftsman merely added secondary chipping (also called retouching) to one or more of its edges. This gave the flake a durable cutting edge suitable for skinning animals, scaling fish, etc. Almost any stone flake (thrown off in implement making) could be chipped and used as a knife, regardless of its size or what sort of material it was. Flake knives are found in great numbers in Delaware.

GORGES

The gorge is made from animal bone. It is three or four inches in length and has two pointed ends. It is believed that gorges were used as fishhooks, having been fastened by their middle to a line and baited on the two ends. Gorges have been found to date only in Sussex County.

GORGETS

Gorgets are thin flat tablets of stone, frequently rectangular in shape and pierced with two or more perforations. They are also known as pierced tablets. The gorget, like the bannerstone and birdstone, is a problematical object and no proved use for it is known.

The word "gorget" connotes an ornament that was worn at the throat or on the breast, but it is not definite that the gorget was so worn. Some archaeologists think that the gorget was a roach spreader or hair ornament. Living tribes are known to use such a device.

Many gorgets have been found in Delaware, mostly of slate. Some of these bear crude designs in the form of incised lines. Others are notched on one or more edges. Because of their fragile nature, gorgets found on the surface are usually broken. Often the broken half is found to be reworked so that it could be used over again.

GOUGES

Gouges are celt-like tools, having one deeply concave surface at the cutting edge. They may have been hafted, or used unhafted in the hand, as a gouging tool. Gouges are extremely rare in Delaware. The few specimens found probably should be called gouge-like celts, because they are not as specialized as the true gouge.

HAMMERSTONES

The Indian used the hammerstone as a hand hammer in implement making. Hammerstones are very common in Delaware. Many of them have a single finger pit in the center of one surface. Others have two finger pits, one on the top and the other at the bottom, to facilitate holding. Cylindrical and triangular hammerstones have also been found. These are always battered on the edges from contact with hard stones. Almost any pebble could be used as a hammerstone. When it broke in use, it was discarded and another taken to replace it.

HOES

Stone hoes are not plentiful in Delaware, although specimens have been found, especially on larger sites, where it may be assumed that agriculture was practised. The hoe is a flat stone, sharpened on one end and notched for hafting to a forked stick. It was used for cultivating corn in much the same way that modern hoes are used. Doubtless the local Indians also used sticks for digging in the soil and hoeing their crops.

LAPSTONES

The lapstone is a stone anvil which was held in the lap as a workbench during the manufacture of stone implements. The typical lapstone, of which scores have been found, is a flat oval or circular boulder about eight or ten inches in diameter. It usually bears scars or peck marks on one or often on two sides, usually in the center of the object. The lapstone is not a showy specimen and is often overlooked by the amateur.

MAULS

The stone maul might be compared to a sledge hammer used for wielding heavy blows. The Delaware maul is a large gravel or pebble, oval in shape, with an encircling groove to permit fastening it to a handle. It does not have a cutting edge.

MORTARS (MILLING STONES)

The stone mortar was a receptacle made to hold corn during the process of grinding it into meal. The common Delaware specimen is a large flat stone or boulder in which a shallow cup-like depression has been worked. Delaware specimens are never polished and are much cruder than the metates of the Southwest. In fact, Delaware mortars exhibit little workmanship except the central depression, usually pecked in with a hammerstone. Often two depressions are found, one on each surface. Stone mortars are not abundant in Delaware, and there is good evidence that wooden mortars were used by the natives. The stone mortars were probably also used for crushing nuts.

MULLERS

The artifact known to Delaware students as a muller is a pebble large enough to fit the hand, having one flat and one rounded side. The flat side exhibits scars or abrasions, indicating that it was exposed to friction with another stone. It is not unlikely that the muller was used for grinding corn, the kernels being placed on a second stone, or shallow mortar, and rubbed. It may have also been used for grinding acorns and cracking nuts.

NET SINKERS

Net sinkers are ordinary creek pebbles, usually with flat surfaces, which have been notched on two sides to permit being tied to a net. Since almost any stone would serve the purpose of weighing down his net, the Indian took no particular pains in the manufacture of the sinker. Net sinkers are found throughout Delaware, especially on the river sites, but are frequently overlooked by the amateur in search of more spectacular specimens.

The larger net sinkers are thought by some to have been canoe weights or anchors. It is difficult to say whether the specimen was used as an anchor or a weight, except that the larger objects would seem to have been appropriate for such application.

PAINT POTS

The Indians are known to have mixed colored pigments in tiny receptacles before applying the color to their faces. Francis Jordan, as previously mentioned, found a paint pot of shell at Rehoboth. Small receptacles made of stone were also used for mixing paint, but they are not common in Delaware. I have seen a number of such receptacles made of steatite which were excavated with Indian burials near Cambridge, Maryland.

PENDANTS, STONE

The stone pendant is a small flat ornament, usually circular or oval, perforated with a single hole. Presumably it was worn as we wear a locket, as a neck ornament. Pendants are not common in Delaware. Some of them were made from broken and reworked gorgets.

PESTLES

To pound corn, pulverize acorns, etc., the Indians used a cylindrical stone object called a roller pestle. Pestles vary in size from small specimens six or eight inches long to others eighteen inches or two feet in length. The smaller specimens are found more frequently in Delaware than the larger ones. Pestles in Delaware are generally crude—they are pecked but seldom polished except at the ends. The bell-shaped pestle is absent in Delaware.

PICKS

In the process of quarrying steatite, the aborigines used stone picks to remove the stone from its natural veins. These picks were fashioned from a hard stone and are crudely made, pointed on one end only. They were seemingly hafted to wooden handles and used as digging tools in much the same way that a modern pick is used. No picks have been found within the Delaware state lines to date, but over the border in Pennsylvania many picks have been found at the steatite quarry near Christiana, already mentioned.

PIPES

Smoking pipes in Delaware are extremely rare. The Smithsonian Institution has in its possession two stone effigy pipes purported to have originated in Delaware, but no site location is known. (An effigy pipe bears on its bowl or stem in bas relief the likeness of a man, animal, or bird.)

From the pipe fragments found on the surface and excavated, it appears that both clay and stone pipes were in use in Delaware. The typical clay pipe is small and crude, having a short stem which meets the bowl at an obtuse angle. Stone pipes appear to have been made of slate and steatite, but in the absence of a series of specimens it is wise to withhold any conclusions pending further work.

PLUMMETS

Among the rare problematical objects are stone plummets, which are similar in appearance to plumb bobs. The writer has seen only one such object in a local collection which was found in Delaware. This specimen was recovered from the surface near Georgetown by Harold T. Purnell.

POTSHERDS

Potsherds are fragments of clay pottery—segments from the neck of the vessel are known as rimsherds. Potsherds are found abundantly in sites in Kent and Sussex Counties, but are not as numerous in New Castle County, although they are sometimes found. Potsherds are easily broken into bits by the plow, and most of the sherds found on cultivated ground are small. There are some exceptions to this rule.

Some unthinking amateurs do not bother to pick up sherds because they are fragmentary and seem of no value. Actually, pottery is more important in the study of a prehistoric people than any other single artifact. Pottery styles and ornamentations are susceptible to change and are criteria of cultural development and change.

In Kent and Sussex counties, more is known about the type of pottery in use by the Indians than in New Castle County. Typical of southern Delaware pottery are vessels with pointed or conoidal bottoms. Round-bottomed vessels were in use, but the pointed bottom seems to have been the prevailing form.

Another characteristic of southern Delaware pottery is the

absence of a collar or overhanging rim on the vessels. The rim is either flush with the sides or turned slightly outward. No collars or rims characteristic of the heavy collars seen on Iroquoian ware have been recorded to date, although no one can guess what might be found in the future.

The exterior bodies of the vessels were marked, so that a roughened exterior resulted. By making casts of the exterior of these vessels we find that the markings were made with cords and nets. These cords were twisted around a wooden paddle, and then used to pat the sides of the wet clay vessel. This caused the clay to knit together more firmly and at the same time left the distinctive markings on the outside.

Many of the vessels are also ornamented near the rims. The design mentioned in the previous paragraph was more for utility than ornament, but the rim designs were purely ornamental. These consist of parallel lines running around the necks: or of triangles used in various design motifs. Rectangular designs are scarce, nor have circular designs been observed. Neither have any resemblances to man, bird, or animal been noted on any of the pottery ornamentation. These designs were merely lines etched in the wet clay by the use of twigs or shells. Punctate ornamentation is not very often found on Delaware vessels.

These vessels are commonly tempered with shells, quartz crystals, or sand. This tempering served as a binder in the clay and made the vessels more durable. The coil method was used in the construction of the pottery. Vessels vary in colors from red, yellow, and gray to those burnt black. They also vary in size from small cup-like containers to vessels eighteen inches high. The large vessels seem to have been used for storage purposes; others were used as cooking pots; and the smallest ones were either drinking cups or children's toys.

Delaware pottery very strongly resembles pottery from New Jersey and Maryland, attesting to the relationship between the natives of this immediate area. It is to be hoped that a comparative study of the pottery from these neighboring states will be made in the near future.

SCRAPERS

The scraper is a tool of chipped stone also known as a "flesher." There is good evidence that it was used to scrape the flesh from animal hides preparatory to tanning. In Delaware the so-called thumb-nail scrapers are common. Found also in great numbers are stemmed scrapers made of broken arrowheads. The broken point has been reworked to a round, spoon-shaped scraping edge, bearing minute secondary chipping.

SEMI-LUNAR KNIVES

The slate knife, or ulu, thought by some authorities to be indicative of influence from the Eskimo, is not a trait in the material culture of Delaware's prehistoric peoples. One semi-lunar knife marked "Delaware" is owned by the University of Pennsylvania Museum. Two broken fragments of semi-lunar knives were found on the Clyde Farm site at Stanton, Delaware, by S. C. Robinson. Delaware apparently lies at the margin of the slate cultures which are prominent in the archaeology of New York State.

SINEW STONES

The sinew stone bears the same relation to the bow string that the arrowshaft smoother does to the shaft. The sinew stone is found in various shapes and its only constant feature is a series of fan-like grooves deeply etched on one or more of its edges. The belief is that the sinews used for bow strings were drawn through these grooves to prepare them for use on the bow. Although present on Delaware sites, the sinew stone is not common.

STEATITE VESSELS

Throughout Delaware, fragments of steatite (soapstone) vessels are found on Indian sites. Steatite is more prevalent in Kent and Sussex counties than it is in New Castle County. The Museum of the American Indian in New York City owns two steatite vessels found in Delaware. Local collectors have portions of other vessels. Delaware steatite vessels have the usual lug handles, and specimens were rounded, oval, or rectangular in shape, very similar to steatite vessels of Tidewater Virginia. Because of its unique resistance to heat, the steatite vessel was used for cooking. Because of its softness, it could be readily hewn to the desired shape with stone chisels.

STONE TUBES

The stone tube, which is a trait of some of the Midwestern mound cultures, is a rarity in Delaware. The writer has never found such a specimen, nor has he been present when one was found. One specimen of a beautiful stone tube, collected by the late James Banning, was purported to have been dug up near Wilmington at the Malleable Iron Works many years ago. It was in association with one perfect gorget and two large spear points made of Ohio flint. These are at this writing on display at the Archaeological Museum at the University of Delaware.

TRADE PIPES

Smoking pipes of white clay were used in Delaware by the Swedes, Dutch, and English. Some of these pipes were of the church warden type, having long stems and elongated bowls. Doubtless many of these pipes were traded with the Indians. Hundreds of fragments of these white European pipes have been picked up on the surface of Delaware Indian sites. The writer has found at least one hundred of these fragments some of which are marked on the stems with the initials of their makers, which may eventually serve to identify the country of their origin. To date, none of the trade pipes has been excavated in association with Indian materials in Delaware. Consequently it is untrue to state positively that they were smoked by the Indians until such evidence comes to light, as it well might in the future. It is always possible that these pipes were used by the early white colonists, although in neighboring states archaeologists have proved through finding the pipes in Indian graves that they were traded to the natives.

*   *   *

The foregoing descriptions do not adequately classify every type of specimen reported from local sites. Objects which defy specific use classification have been found, and any collector is proud to exhibit one or more oddities in his cabinet which are unlike the prevailing forms. A word of caution is necessary: the wise student will refrain from making positive statements regarding the original use of specimens of Indian manufacture unless he has substantial proof of his claim. In archaeology, as in most sciences, the more one learns the less he finds he knows, and the majority of professional archaeologists today are inclined to avoid guesswork.

Fortunately, most of the largest collections of Delaware artifacts are still available within the state for further study as needed; the most representative collection is now on exhibit at the Archaeological Museum, University of Delaware. Surprisingly few of the nation's large museums own collections of Delaware artifacts, and those with the largest collection are listed below in the order of the size of their Delaware material:

Peabody Museum of Archaeology and Ethnology, Harvard University, Cambridge, Mass.
Museum of the American Indian, Heye Foundation, New York City.
United States National Museum, Smithsonian Institution, Washington, D.C.
University Museum, University of Pennsylvania, Philadelphia.
Bucks County Historical Society, Doylestown, Penna.
American Museum of Natural History, New York City.

Students of Delaware artifacts may be interested in knowing that the first Indian relic collector in the state was none other than the pot-bellied Swede, Governor Johan Printz. On July 19,

1644, three hundred years ago, Printz wrote as follows from New Sweden in a letter addressed to Tycho Brahe in Europe describing Indian specimens he was sending to Queen Christina:

I have often thought of my Royal Majesty, my most gracious Queen, to present her with some strange gift, in highest humility, but could not find anything special until now, except one of the foremost bands [made of beads] which the Indian chiefs use on their Kinteks and greatest glory, and is so highly esteemed among them as among us gold and silver. The black is counted as gold, the white as silver. I also send a tobacco pipe which the Savages have themselves made of stone, from which her Royal Majesty can graciously see what the best gifts and splendor of the Savages are, as well as how artistic they are, not only in wood, but also in stone and on other metals to do and to work. I have nothing special which I can present to your Excellency except a Savage tobacco pipe of wood and an Indian otter skin muff which I request humbly that your Excellency may not think amiss of your poor servant.

In summation, the material culture of the aboriginal people of Delaware, as shown by the specimens that have been excavated or found on the surface of the ground, presents certain individualities that make strong contrasts with the artifacts found in other parts of the United States. A detailed comparison would require technical analysis that would be out of place in this story, but even the casual reader may be curious to know how Delaware fits in the national fabric of native handiwork. From a broad view it can be said that the abundance, variety, and quality of workmanship of the implements of polished and chipped stone is the foremost trait in the material culture of the local aborigines. They sought and utilized every known source of stone within reach, and were past masters in stone-working techniques. It is this factor that emphasizes their stone-age role in American history. The grooved axe, cylindrical pestle, shallow mortar, muller, bi-pitted hammerstone, and the wide variety of expertly made arrowheads, scrapers, and cutting tools follow a pattern of stone artifacts that has affinities in Maryland, eastern Pennsylvania and New Jersey. Their bannerstones, gorgets, pendants, and other polished stone ceremonials are superior in workmanship to the stone artifacts made by the Iroquois peoples of New York, but are inferior to similar objects excavated in parts of New England, New Jersey, and in the southeastern states.

Their clay pottery vessels, while artistically made and highly practical from a utility viewpoint, are not as graceful or durable as the vessels made by natives in many other areas. Their clay vessels are inferior, for example, to the pottery manufactured by their contemporary neighbors living on the Susquehanna River whose ceramic ware was characterized by large, highly decorated collars and flaring rims, which required the greatest of skill. Indeed, one who has studied the pottery of the Susquehannock carefully as weighed against that of Delaware would come to the conclusion that the latter people were trying to imitate their neighbors' techniques. Once again one sees distinct similarities between Delaware pottery and that found in Maryland, New Jersey, eastern Pennsylvania and some parts of Virginia, which is suggestive of a cultural kinship. Nevertheless none of this Eastern ware, Delaware included, can approach the fine-textured painted vessels made by native groups of the great American Southwest, accepted as the highest advanced form of potter's art on this continent.

The simple, angular clay smoking pipes found sparingly in Delaware may not be compared in style and beauty with the stone platform pipes excavated in the Ohio and Mississippi valleys which are also among the most highly-rated examples of primitive stone industry in America.

The artifacts of bone, antler, and shell made by the earliest Delawareans, which as we have seen were manufactured sparingly, sink into insignificance when contrasted with the exquisite bone work of some of the New York Iroquoian peoples who used bone and antler as extensively as the Delaware folk employed stone. Even among other related woodland tribes, as for instance the natives of the Monongahela drainage system in Western Pennsylvania, Dr. Mary Butler and George Fisher have disclosed that they were far more proficient in working in bone and antler than the tribes of Delaware. Conversely, the Monongahela folk were less proficient in stone-working.

All things considered, New Jersey produces material closest in type to the artifacts found in Delaware. Yet the carved stone faces and sculptured heads, some fetishes and others ornaments, which have been recorded from New Jersey are totally absent to date in Delaware.

Except for a few crude copper beads, metal artifacts were unknown in Delaware, and in this connection the natives of Central America, who made extensive use of silver and gold, were far more advanced. The reader must also remember that none of the tribes in the eastern Atlantic region practised extensive metal working, so little distinction can be made regarding Delaware.

From this very superficial comparison, one infers that the Indians of Delaware hold an intermediate position in the ranks of early American craftsmen, based entirely on archaeological remains. They were neither the best nor the worst. Geographically they were also in an intermediate position occupying a region lying between the northern and southern peoples where they could feel influences from either direction. Their homes also lay in lands drained by two major waterways—the Chesapeake on the west and the Delaware on the east—and as a border territory, influences were brought to bear from both sides. Archaeologically, Delaware's importance is due to this position which permitted its occupants to live within range of many surrounding tribes and to feel the waves of cultural diffusion that came from north, south, east, and west.

In further summary, the principal aboriginal remains of Delaware which have survived may, as we have seen, be grouped into the following divisions: camp and village sites, fishing stations, shell heaps, rock shelters, ossuaries, graves, fish weirs, and caches. Similar features are found in other coastal states; so Delaware has nothing extraordinary in this direction to offer.

The general absence of suitable stone for implement making because of the nature of the state's geological deposits accounts for the absence of aboriginal quarries. In this respect Delaware stands out from most eastern states where quarries have been located, but this record may not last. Recently we have noticed that a type of ferruginous quartz is present in large veins below the surface of the ground on Iron Hill, near Newark. Furthermore, arrowheads made of the identical stone are distributed on sites at the foot of the hill on the upper branches of the Christina River. It is not unlikely that the Indians may have obtained the quartz, which is of a distinctive sorrel color, by quarrying the vein on the hill. If so, the quarry may someday be found.

Throughout Delaware traces of old Indian trails remained through the colonial period but have since been obliterated. They were narrow, unmarked footpaths, worn deep by the tread of countless feet through the forests that separated one native town or camp from others. The best known of these old trails was called the Choptank, or Delaware, Indian path, and its route was marked on the deeds of properties which it crossed. The historian William B. Marye, a resident of Baltimore and a painstaking scholar of land records, traced this trail by studying the early documents and collating the references to the trail. He learned that it started at New Castle and crossed the state to Back Creek, a tributary of Elk River. Then it followed the shore of Chesapeake Bay in a southerly direction, crossing over fording places on the Chester and Sassafras rivers, finally terminating at the Indian towns on the Choptank and Nanticoke rivers. From here another important trail crossed the tangled forest to Lewes, joining the villages on Delaware Bay.

The present highway connecting Wilmington with Marcus Hook, Claymont, Chester, and Philadelphia was formerly an Indian path; the Lancaster Pike and the Newport Pike were also laid on Indian trails. The network of narrow paths served the natives as arteries of commerce, along with the navigable streams, just as our modern highways accommodate the tourist. Few people today stop to think that the Indian trails were the forerunners of our cement roads, just as the Indian towns were the sites of our cities.

As yet there is no record in Delaware of petroglyphs, or pic-

Pottery vessels excavated from shell pits at Slaughter Creek

Rock shelter (*above*) and remains of fish weir (*below*), Doe Run, discovered by the author

tographs, as they are also called, which are designs representing animals, birds, and other figures scratched on the surface of boulders or rock outcroppings. Pictographs are frequently found along the banks of streams navigated by the Indians. A series of unusual pictographs were removed from an island in the Susquehanna River a few years ago by Pennsylvania archaeologists when the Safe Harbor Dam was under construction. The pictures cut in the rocks are difficult to decipher and probably relate a story or legend which we are yet unable to interpret. Archaeologists have carefully sought pictographs along Delaware's rockiest stream, the Brandywine, where they would logically be expected to be situated. Up to the present the search has been fruitless, and this is a conspicuous missing link in Delaware archaeology.

Formerly there were numerous traces of fish weirs in the Brandywine, not made of logs like Cresson's structure in Naaman's Creek, but constructed of large pebbles and boulders. These stone dams extended from shore to shore, in V shape, with the apex pointed downstream. These weirs were constructed to block the passage of shad as they attempted to return to the sea after spawning upstream, permitting the natives to catch them in great numbers.

A few years ago I was fortunate in locating an old unrecorded fish weir on Doe Run, a branch of the Brandywine, which is believed to have been constructed by the early Indians. Enough of the original boulders remain to trace the lines of the old weir from one bank to the other, although many of the stones have washed away. Dr. Maurice Mook, an anthropologist who was later affiliated with the American University in Washington, D.C., assisted in making some archaeological explorations in the bed of the stream. Unfortunately we were not able to locate any artifacts which might be attributed to the native fishermen. Occupational traces, however, were found on the floor of a rock shelter along the north bank of the stream, and we were led to believe that the fishermen camped in this convenient shelter. The locations of several other apparent rock shelters along the Brandywine have been noted for future investigation. Because of the absence of rock outcroppings south of Wilmington, it is unlikely that similar shelters will be found elsewhere in the state.

Periodical reports arise in Delaware of the finding of mounds which purport to be identical with the tumuli of the Midwest. Such reports have always proved thus far to be erroneous. Investigation always has revealed that the rumor was caused by attention being drawn to a hillock or knoll which resembled a mound in shape, but was the result of natural causes. I personally have been party to a dozen or more wild goose chases in search of non-existent mounds. One such mound hunt was prompted by an article appearing in the January 1879 issue of the *American Antiquarian* which came to attention a few years ago, long after it had originally been published. A short excerpt reprinted in the journal was quoted as an extract from the Wilmington *Sunday Star* of 1879. The article called attention to the discovery of an Indian mound near Wilmington from which human bones had been removed. This excited our interest, and using the article as a guide we strove unsuccessfully to find the place where the mound had supposedly been found. Finally we decided to investigate the article itself in its original context, and imagine our surprise to learn that the first issue of the Wilmington *Sunday Star* appeared in 1881, fully two years after the article was supposed to have appeared. This complicated the issue even further, and finally the newspaper files at the Library of Congress were minutely combed. There we found the answer. I learned that the article had originally been published in the Wilmington North Carolina *Star*, and accurately described a mound found in the environs of the southern city. The editor of the *Antiquarian* had reprinted the article, but carelessly attributed the excerpt to a non-existent Delaware newspaper. Another archaeological enigma was solved, but we were no closer to finding an Indian mound in Delaware than before.

❖   ❖   ❖

Delaware possesses one unique archaeological phenomenon that has never been properly studied or explained. Because it is so far back from the well-traveled roads it has been observed by relatively few persons. Perhaps it is premature to discuss it now, but my purpose is merely to record its existence. Near Port Penn, on a marshy branch of the Delaware River, lies a rolling farm which is known to some of the local folk as the Indian Hole Farm. This designation is derived from a series of approximately twenty holes found on a neck of wooded land lying along the northern edge of the farm, about a mile from the house. The strip of land has never been cultivated and rises about ten feet above the water and marsh which surround it on all sides except at the base where it joins the mainland. From the distance it resembles a shady grove of no unusual significance, but as one makes his way down the path running between the oak trees, he sees that the entire area is pocked with holes. The holes vary in depth from two to six feet and in width from six to fifteen feet. Most of them are partially filled with moist leaf mold which has collected over many successive autumns. The grass and other vegetation growing on the inside walls of the holes would indicate that they were not dug in recent times.

When I first stumbled on this farm in 1939 while seeking aboriginal sites along the Delaware River, the property was tenanted by a William Ellis, a most obliging farmer. When I asked Mr. Ellis about the purpose of the holes, he said that he had been told that the Indians once lived in them, covering over the tops with animal skins as a protection against the weather. I pointed out that there is no record of this mode of living among the Indians of the Delaware region, and life in such damp holes would certainly be unhealthful. He admitted the logic of my remarks, but had no other explanation to offer. The holes had been there longer than he could remember and had always been called Indian Holes.

Giving credence to the weight of local tradition, I puttered in the banks of the plot of land, and explored adjacent fields but could find nothing of aboriginal manufacture. The impression was gathered that the holes may have been the remains of quarry pits where, by digging in the earth, the native quarrymen obtained pebbles for use in making their implements. Quarries of this type were found not far distant from Washington, D.C., by the late W. H. Holmes along with tremendous quantities of stone chips, quarry blanks, rejectage, and incomplete artifacts. Similar quarry pits are known in Berks County, Pennsylvania, where the Indians dug holes in the ground to obtain jasper, and here too the earth in the vicinity of the pits is littered with stone rejectage. But no stone flakes, rejectage, spalls, blanks, or any other lithic clues to a quarrying industry are present at Indian Hole Farm.

The thought also occurred to me that the pits may have resulted from the Indians digging for clay to be used in the manufacture of pottery vessels. The opinions of other local archaeological students were sought, and several visits were made to the Indian Holes in their company, but no one could offer any reasonable theories. Subsequently we planned a digging project to determine if through excavational techniques it might fall our fortune to find a solution to the riddle. Alas, on our next visit, we learned that Mr. Ellis no longer occupied the farm and new tenants had moved in. They were adamant in their attitude, and refused pointblank not only to permit us to dig, but would not even consent to our walking over the property. This project, therefore, must also await a future opportunity. In the meantime, one grows restless as he meditates on the strange Indian Holes. Were they dug by the Indians? Or are they the result of some commercial venture of white men which has long been forgotten?

10.

Where Did the Indians Originate?

As WE have seen, all reliable archaeological evidence found to date in Delaware points to its first occupancy by a relatively late prehistoric people whom we call Indians. Where did the Indians come from? How long did they occupy Delaware? Were they preceded by a pre-Indian people? These questions have provoked more than one flight into the realm of imagination. Some of the early colonists thought the Indians were members of the lost tribes of Israel, and even William Penn argued that the Indian language was related to the Semitic tongues. Others insisted that the Indians were people of the lost continent of Atlantis who had survived after their homes had sunk into the ocean. Many other equally unsound notions were accepted as truth although they lacked the weight of scientific proof. Fortunately we are closer to the correct answer today than ever before, and as our investigations continue we shall be able to close the gaps in our knowledge.

First we must discount any notions that man developed in Delaware from a lower form of life. In fact, lack of evidence for forerunners of a primitive type anywhere in the Western Hemisphere precludes any supposition that man developed here, although some people will still argue the point. If the Indian did not develop in America, then where was his place of origin? Was he a descendant of the Jews or the offshoot of some obscure island cultural group? The answer is flatly no.

The marked similarity in physical structure and features between the American Indians and Eastern Asiatics, as well as certain cultural resemblances, first suggested a common heritage.

149

Pursuing this point of reasoning, anthropologists have come to agree that the ancestors of the historic Indians came to America from Asia, and that they were the first human occupants of this continent. There is some difference of opinion regarding the migratory routes over which these Asiatic people came, but the majority of scientists working on the problem consider the Bering Strait region as the most likely avenue, especially for the earliest movement. Archaeological work in Asia and northwestern America, which is yet far from complete, supports this theory. The date of arrival of the first Asiatic immigrants has long been a perplexing problem, and opinions have shifted from one extreme to the other, from millions of years to a few thousand years, the latter too recent to be accepted in view of the indisputable evidence to the contrary which we shall presently examine.

Students of living Indian tribes have come to believe that the several apparent physical types found among the Indians, the diverse languages, and difference in cultural properties and ceremonies show a long interval of separation from their former home in the Orient. In seeking the origins of America's first occupants, there was a great vogue for the finding of the remains of paleolithic man in America, following the announcement of his occurrence in Europe. The Delaware River valley received its full share of attention in this quest which was destined to fail. For a long time following the controversy involving Abbott, Putnam, Holmes, Volk, Mercer, Cresson, and others a feeling of distrust pervaded scientific circles when ancient man was discussed. The topic was almost taboo, and was avoided as much as possible, although the search in America quietly continued. Then in 1925 reputable scientists with long experience produced conclusive evidence of the existence of a people in the West of greater antiquity than is usually assigned to the Indians.

At Folsom, New Mexico, in the little valley of a tributary to the Cimarron River, excavators uncovered the skeletons of a herd of bison. The bones of bulls, cows and calves were lying close together under about fifteen feet of earth, where they had obviously lain for centuries. Their positions suggested that the herd had gathered at a water hole and were struck down by hunters. Most of the animals' tail bones were missing, hinting further at the work of human hands that removed the tails. Far more conclusive of man's presence were a number of chipped dart points mixed with the animal bones, the instruments that had caused their death.

The most significant point of the discovery was that the bison remains were not those of the *Bison Americanus* which roamed the plains in the historic period, but were the bones of *Bison Taylori*, an animal which is believed to have become extinct on the American continent between fifteen thousand and twenty-five thousand years ago. The stone darts found mingled with the bones of the extinct bison were new to archaeologists. They were of a distinctive type, having a longitudinal channel or fluting on each face different from the typical Indian stone arrowhead. These points, which were probably fastened to javelins, were given the name Folsom Points, and archaeologists set about to find others like them in similar settings.

Later, near Fort Collins, Colorado, a camping place that had been frequented by Folsom hunters was found, and subsequently other sites were located in the West. The distinctive fluted Folsom points were uncovered in direct association not only with the bones of the extinct bison, but intermingled with the remains of extinct mammoth, American camel, musk ox, ground sloth, and antelope. Some of the Folsom points were observed imbedded in the bones of the extinct creatures, certain proof that man was contemporary with the animals.

We know very little about the mode of life of these early Folsom men and less about their appearance. They left behind no traces of pottery or agriculture, and we are led to assume that they were itinerant hunters. We cannot be sure that they used bows and arrows, for, as intimated, the Folsom point may have been a spear tip, the people not yet having reached the advanced stage of the bow and arrow. If so, it is clear that the Folsom hunter ran down his game on foot, matching his wits against animals fleeter on foot than he and far mightier in strength and endurance. Judged by our standards, he was an ignorant savage, yet he must have been wise in the ways of nature, and far shrewder and more resourceful than any of the beasts he hunted. Dr. Frank H. H. Roberts, Jr., one of the archaeologists of the United States Bureau of American Ethnology specializing in the study of what has become known as the Folsom Complex, thinks of Folsom man as a paleo-Indian arriving in the New World from Asia approximately fifteen thousand years ago with a culture comparable to the Late Neolithic or Early Paleolithic in Europe, using those terms in their broadest sense. So while Dr. Abbott's pre-Indian man of the Delaware Valley is still a myth, the Folsom hunters rate an antiquity in America consonant with his theories. Future research may, of course, reveal the existence in America of a people who were here prior to the coming of Folsom man.

Returning to the archaeology of Delaware, there is record of ten projectile or dart points, similar in general type to the western Folsom points, having been found on the surface of the ground in the state. They are not true Folsom points, but may be classed as Folsom-like, and present a problem of great interest. In the Far West, the range of Folsom man's wanderings has been established by the places where the points are found. The finding of points somewhat similar must not be construed to mean that Folsom peoples came this far east, but it is a possibility that cannot be discounted without having more evidence than is now at hand. Some authorities think it more feasible that the Folsom-like points distributed in Delaware and other eastern states may be aberrant types made by the Indians in imitation of the older type which they may have tried to duplicate.

To avoid any misunderstanding, let us reiterate that according to the best archaeological evidence produced in Delaware, the earliest occupants appeared on the scene sometime long after the last glacier returned to the far north. They lived in a well-developed stone culture, practised agriculture, and made and used pottery. Archaeology as yet has revealed no certain traces of an older pre-pottery or pre-agricultural people, akin to those of the Folsom horizon. Moreover, with the exception of the rock shelter excavated by Cresson, which is not admissible as proof because of the doubts expressed as to its authenticity, there are as yet no records of stratified sites having been found within the borders of the state. All evidence now at hand, which is admittedly not conclusive and is based on incomplete archaeological work, seems to point in the direction of a primitive people with a homogeneous culture occupying the waterways throughout the state.

In southern Delaware, where aboriginal sites are larger, more numerous, and more productive of artifacts, the people were essentially coastal, deriving much of their food from the water. They also practised agriculture, but seemingly were not great hunters. In northern Delaware, the native residents were also a semi-sedentary fishing and agricultural people, but presumably were not as numerous as the southern folk, nor were they as dependent upon shellfish for food.

In other eastern states, notably New York, archaeologists have worked out a chronological sequence of occupation from excavating many stratified sites, revealing the presence of successive groups of Indians from the oldest nomadic people whose culture was in many ways archaic down to the advanced Iroquois cultures of the historic era. Dr. William Ritchie, in his studies of Iroquois and pre-Iroquois sites in New York, has made outstanding contributions in this direction, but the time sequence in his area does not apply to Delaware and related coastal regions. Further archaeological work in Delaware must be launched so that the state can stand on her own feet in the scientific world. Research here to be valid must necessarily include the entire Delmarva Peninsula, as a single archaeological unit, irrespective of state lines. A wealth of material and information awaits the investigator on this peninsula, most of which still remains unexplored. The land surface has just been scratched.

11.

Conclusion

IN STRIVING to interpret the problems of the past, the archaeologist never allows himself to lose sight of the fact that history can be of invaluable aid to him. History is the starting point from which he works back with spade and trowel, as he delves into more shadowy problems. Knowledge of the first historical records pertaining to a native people, even though the account is not always to be relied upon as strictly accurate in all details, constitutes the written preface to an unwritten chapter. He knows that the Indians living in Delaware at the time of discovery were following a pattern of living that originated in past ages with their ancestors. Through perusal of the early documents and relations, he learns that the tawny peoples of northern Delaware first referred to themselves not as Indians, but as Lenni Lenape. In their language this term meant "original men" or "real men." After contact with the whites, the Lenape came to be called Delaware Indians, a name derived from Lord de La Warr, an Englishman, which was also given to the bay, river, and eventually the state.

A traditional history of the Lenni Lenape was preserved among the members of the tribe and handed down to their descendants. The story was recorded by means of crude pictures painted on sticks, known as the Walum Olum. According to those who have interpreted the Walum Olum, the Lenape in late prehistoric times came from the west or northwest, crossed the Mississippi River, then continued eastward until they arrived in what is now Pennsylvania. After a while they divided their forces. Some of their number settled in eastern Pennsylvania, northern Delaware, and New Jersey. Others moved down Chesapeake Bay, probably by boat, and made their homes along the waterways of the Delmarva Peninsula (also on the western shore of Maryland) and formed independent bands, tribes, and family groups. If this account can be accepted as authentic, then the Nanticoke Indians and the Assateague (who settled on Indian River in Sussex County about 1700 after having been driven from their home at "Buckingham," Maryland) as well as the many unidentified bands who lived at Lewes, Rehoboth, Slaughter Creek, and elsewhere in southern Delaware, all stemmed from the same family root as the Lenape. Here we lean on ethnohistory to corroborate the fact that there were pronounced similarities in the languages, religious practices, and social organizations of all these Algonkian-speaking peoples which tends to support the assumption of a common ancestry.

Therefore, if we accept the Walum Olum, this would mean that Delaware was populated by a wave of Algonkian-speaking peoples who entered the state principally from the north, and archaeological remains tend to confirm this belief. This does not preclude the possibility that there may also have been an entrance of like peoples from the southwest via Virginia and Chesapeake Bay into the Delmarva Peninsula, a supposition that must await archaeological work in the almost virgin southernmost parts of the peninsula. Since the natives of Delaware were affiliated with the Algonkian family, let us pause for a few remarks about these Indians as substantiated by history.

The Algonkian peoples were not only the first to welcome the Swedish and Dutch settlers in Delaware, and the English in Virginia and Maryland, but their relatives in New England and on Manhattan Island were the first Indians to greet the whites. A numerous family, they held most of the country east of the Mississippi from Tennessee on the south to Hudson's Bay in the north. Clark Wissler, in his epochal work *Indians of the United States,* says that the most famous individual Indians in our early history were eastern Algonkians; for example, Pocahontas, Powhatan, Massasoit, King Philip, Tamanend, and others. There were also Algonkian tribes who lived on the great plains, in the central area and in the far West, but they are not now of immediate interest to us. Among the Algonkians on the Atlantic slope, we find the Lenape, Nanticoke, Choptank, Abnaki, Mahican, Massachusetts, Micmac, Montagnais, Narraganset, Naskapi, Pequot, Pohatan tribes, and Wampanoag, to name the most important.

Prior to the coming of the Europeans, a southern Indian family, the Iroquois, had crept up into the Algonkian territory, centralizing their strength in New York state. Many Algonkians lost their lives resisting this invasion from the south, and a war was still being waged between the two peoples when the whites appeared on the scene in 1500 to 1600. The Iroquois formed a confederacy of Five Nations (later the Six Nations) which became so strong that they were able to subdue many of the Algonkian tribes, forcing them to accept the status of tributary nations.

The Algonkian weakness was their inability to unify their full strength against the invader or they undoubtedly could have exterminated him. The many bands, tribes, and family groups, despite their traditional language and cultural ties, existed independently like tiny nations. This is one of the chief reasons why the Iroquois were able to force their way up along the Appalachians to the north, and why the Algonkians, including the Lenape and Nanticoke of Delaware, fell an easy prey to them. This background picture gives the archaeologist the perspective needed to aid him in reconstructing the probable events that occurred before the advent of the white man in America.

The handiwork of the Algonkians is distributed in the soil throughout the vast area where they lived. In northern Delaware the Lenni Lenape and their ancestors were responsible for the stone and clay artifacts found so abundantly, which often reflect the influence of the Iroquois on the Alongkian culture. According to the journals of the earliest Europeans to visit the Delaware region, the Lenape population center along the western shore of the Delaware River in 1600 was in the environs of present Philadelphia. On the Schuylkill River were located two permanent villages, or towns, called Passayung and Nittabonck. On the banks of the Delaware not far away were the villages called Poaetquessingh, Pemickpacka, Wickquauenscke, Wickquackonick, Sipaessingh, and probably others. Each village, according to Peter Lindeström, a Swedish engineer who visited among the tribes in 1654, had its separate chieftain. The sachem of the largest and most important village at Passayung exercised authority over the other chiefs as a "king." As the English settled at Philadelphia and a city began to take shape, the natives were driven away and their villages were eventually buried under cobbled streets and dwellings before the dawn of archaeological research in America.

Only two Lenape villages are definitely cited by name in the territory south of Philadelphia. One called Minguannan was on White Clay Creek near the Old London Tract Church, and another called Queominising was located on the great bend of the Brandywine, partly in Pennsylvania and partly in Delaware. Neither site has been excavated.

Many Indian names of Algonkian extraction may be seen on old maps, such as Hopokohacking, and Wawaset near present Wilmington; Amimenipoty near Edgemoor; Memomkitonna at Claymont; Hwiskakimensi at Newport, and others. Concrete documentary proof is lacking that these names applied to native villages. More likely they were place names which the Indians commonly gave to rivers, creeks, hills, swamps, and other topographical features.

The white explorers and missionaries who associated with the Lenape while they still dwelt in the Delaware Valley tell us that there were three main subdivisions in the tribe; the Minsi, Unami, and Unalachtigo. These terms were said to mean, respectively: people of the stony country; people down the river; people living near the ocean. Each of the three subtribes, in turn, contained clans whose animal totems were wolf, turkey, and turtle. Some historians have gone so far as to assign one or the other of these specific clans to Delaware, but it is not certain which of them actually occupied the state because of the absence of authentic contemporary accounts relating to the tribal subdivisions. Apart from this debatable question of identity, the early explorers have left a fairly comphrensive story of the customs and habits of the Lenape which is helpful in interpreting archaeological findings. Because of the availability of many eyewitness accounts, we are able to compare one with the other in evaluating the truthfulness of the observer. Many of the scribes went to great pains to describe certain aboriginal tools and their uses, and these descriptions help to identify some of the artifacts we find today.

Also along the Nanticoke River (in southern Delaware and on the Eastern Shore of Maryland) south of the Lenape domain, there were at least ten Indian villages at the time of the first settlement by the English. We have the names of only five of them, thanks to Captain John Smith, who visited the Nanticoke villages in 1608. They were called Nautaquack, Nause, Saropinagh, Arseek, and Kuskarawaoke. Smith also gave the name of the last-named village to the river which subsequently became known as the Nanticoke.

One of the largest of the Nanticoke Indian villages lay along Broad Creek at the site of Laurel, Delaware, but its Indian name has not been preserved. The occupants of this and the other villages roamed through southern Delaware to hunt and fish at certain times of the year, returning to their homes when the time came to sow their corn, beans, and other agricultural products. Many of the Indian relics found in this territory, particularly along the Nanticoke River at Laurel, Vienna, and other towns on its banks, and along the Marshy Hope Creek and elsewhere in its drainage system, are products of the Nanticoke Indians. Less has been recorded in history about the customs of the Nanticoke than the Lenape, and practically nothing was written by contemporary observers to describe the types of artifacts they used. The tribe were reported to be sorcerers and poisoners, capable of directing their magic arts against their enemies. They were proficient basket makers, according to Captain John Smith, and also produced large quantities of shell beads. He tells us that they were great

traders, having established commerce with other tribes, and we also know that they were one of the tribes to practise the strange chiacason house and ossuary type of burial previously described.

Lewes is built on the site of a former native town which was a large community recorded in history under the name Checonnessex or Sikonesses. The scribes who preserved the name of this village and observed that the resident natives cultivated extensive cornfields neglected to name the tribe that occupied the village. In the Maryland records a statement is found to the effect that the occupants of the town were not Nanticokes, and it is entirely possible that they have have been one of the Lenape bands. If so, this would be the deepest southern penetration of the tribe. Unfortunately the streets of Lewes have destroyed all clues to the Indian town, or its tribal identity may have been established by archaeology. Several years ago, workmen grading for a tennis court near the Lewes school unearthed an Indian burial with their horse-drawn scoop shovel, and later a second grave was found near the old grist mill at the Pennsylvania Station by a man digging holes for his fence posts. All of the bones were too badly crushed to be of scientific value. Kenneth Givan has found many camp sites along the fresh-water streams on the outskirts of Lewes which were probably hunting stations of the people living in the main village. Unfortunately the artifacts found on these minor sites do not give a sufficiently complete cultural picture to justify conclusions.

There were many other villages scattered throughout Delaware, particularly in Kent and Sussex counties, which were not seen by white explorers or were deserted before settlers appeared in the region. Furthermore, we also must not discount the possibility that the explorers may have known of villages which they failed to mention in their writings. Such things were not thought to be of any significance in the early days. Despite the absence of reference in historical accounts, it has been definitely ascertained through archaeology that such

villages existed. In this respect, archaeology is a more reliable divining rod than history. The tangible proof which the soil produces cannot be refuted.

To the early writers and to modern ethnologists working among tribal descendants we are indebted also for information that cannot be obtained by digging in the soil. Such data relate to customs, languages, ceremonies, and religious beliefs. Many of these concepts current at the time of the first contact had been passed down orally from one generation to another. They reveal to us some understanding of the thoughts and beliefs that were present in the primitive mind.

We have already made a brief, superficial comparison between the archaeological specimens found in Delaware and those of near-by states to give the reader a general perspective of the relative position of the inhabitants based on their material culture. To round out this comparison, it would also be necessary to measure the ethnology of the Delaware groups against others of the American tribes, a task of such scope that it would require a lengthier discussion than these pages or the present author's ability allow. Nevertheless it can be said and readily illustrated that anything the Delaware peoples lacked in their artifact technique was compensated for in their mythology. By mythology, which differed from tribe to tribe, we mean a combination of their allegorical fiction, philosophy, mysticism, and ethics. Among the Lenape, to cite only one of many Algonkian-speaking peoples, it was outstanding and well developed, contrary to the popular impression of Indians as ignorant pagans.

For example, the reader may be surprised to learn that the Lenape were deeply religious in their devotion to creeds of the tribe. Their religious beliefs were far more complicated than many modern sects, and here we lean upon the studies of Dr. Speck and M. R. Harrington, cited in the bibliography at the end of this chapter, for the following data.

Regarded by many other tribes as venerable "grandfathers," the Lenape enjoyed the honor of being credited with possessing unusual wisdom and spiritual power. According to their

religion, they thought of the world as the back of a gigantic land turtle. Their legends taught them that many years ago there was nothing but water everywhere on the earth. Then a huge turtle came up out of the sea. As the water fell from his back, a tree took root on it. The tree sent up a sprout and the sprout grew into a man. A second sprout appeared on the tree and became a woman. Thus, according to their philosophy, we have the origin of life, a marine Garden of Eden with an Indian Adam and Eve.

The Lenape acknowledged the existence of a great god or supreme force whom they called Manito. They were taught to believe that he made the world, sun, moon, stars, plants, animals, and all living things. They also believed that there were twelve other Gods (twelve was a sacred number to them; the same number of plates as on the carapace of the turtle) who assisted the great Manito and who were called Manito-wuk. They also believed there were twelve heavens, one lying above the other with a different Manito-wuk living in each. Manito lived in the highest heaven and ruled over all. When the Lenape prayed, they shouted twelve times so that all the Manito-wuk would hear their prayers and repeat them for the benefit of Manito. They recognized Manito as a great and bountiful God who loved them and made the world for the benefit of all the things that lived in it. There were many other gods, or spirit forces, of lesser importance who ruled over the plants and animals. Thunder was considered a mighty spirit who dwelt in the mountains, and who was called an Elder Brother. Another force, the Snow Boy, was a spirit who controlled the snow and ice. Gifts were made to him so that he would give the Indians the proper amount of snow for tracking animals during the winter. The sun, moon, and stars were also considered as separate deity forces and were termed Elder Brothers. From time to time, ceremonies and festivals were held for these gods in which the participants danced, sang, feasted, and offered presents in return for blessings they had received.

According to modern definitions, the Lenape would be

called pagan because their religious concepts included a belief in spirits and supernatural forces and influences emanating from nature. When a boy reached the age of about twelve years his parents thought that he required one of these spirit forces to help guide him through the maze of life. They would urge him to go into the forest alone so that a spirit or one of the Manito-wuk might find him. His parents frequently pretended to chase him away from home, hoping that Manito would take pity on him and give him some power or blessing that would help him when he became a man. While he was alone in the woods, the boy did not eat or drink. The more intensely he suffered, the sooner it was hoped that assistance would come to him from the gods. He prayed fervently that a vision or dream would come to him in which Manito would give him a guardian spirit in the form of a bird, animal, or other natural thing. When he grew up, he could rely upon this guardian spirit for favors and assistance in time of need. It was his own personal god, who took an intimate interest in his affairs. The object that came to the lad while he was dreaming or as he enjoyed his vision became his protector for life. Not every Lenape male was blessed with a guardian spirit. Those so favored often became prominent among the tribe and were regarded with great respect. As part of their religion, the children were taught that the earth and its animals, plants, stars, winds, seasons, rains, and snows were generally friendly to them. But they feared them when people did evil things to make the natural forces angry.

The most important Lenape religious ceremony was held at harvest time when the leaves turned yellow. Those who have studied this ceremony, called the Big House or Gam-Wing, are of the opinion that it dates into the distant past long before any white men approached the shores of the New World. The events took place in a ceremonial structure, similar in feature but larger than the native huts described in an earlier chapter. The ceremony lasted for twelve days, and people from neighboring villages would gather together at a central village to participate.

Inside the Big House, carved on a center pole and on poles along the four walls, were twelve wooden faces. One-half of each face was painted red and the other half black, and they were supposed to represent the faces of the Manito-wuk as the Indians imagined them to look. During the ensuing ceremonies, the men recited the visions that had come to them during boyhood, if they were fortunate enough to possess guardian spirits. Each owned a rattle made from a box turtle which he shook when singing about his vision. Others beat a deerskin drum with sacred drumsticks and repeated the song. Men and women both took part, and some of the women used brushes of turkey wings to keep the Big House free from evil spirits. Birds' feathers were believed to have the property of sweeping away diseases and evil things; and wampum was exchanged as a pledge of good faith. The old women prepared hominy for all the participants to eat. It was a very holy event, and in performing the ceremony the Lenape believed they were pleasing their gods. They prayed for health, immunity from disease and catastrophe; and believed that purity of mind, sincerity, and good moral conduct were necessary to secure an answer to their supplications. Throughout the ceremony, gratitude for the benefits of nature, for life, for health were continually stressed. After completing their songs and dances, they believed they had worshipped everything on earth and that their prayers would help everybody in the world. So deep rooted was the Big House Ceremony in the Indian fiber that it was still held in recent years by "civilized" Lenape Indians living in Oklahoma and Canada.

*   *   *

The foregoing account of a religious episode may seem totally irrelevant in concluding a story of archaeology. Yet these ceremonial and religious practices are a vital part in completing the chronicle of the past. This single example of religion among one of hundreds of native American tribes serves to illustrate the paucity of our knowledge of what occurred before our ancestors arrived in the New World. The stone arrowheads, axes, celts, and pottery that we find today on all sides were made by real, living, breathing people, and are of importance only in so far as they teach us to understand more about their makers. Yes, these people laughed and cried, quibbled among themselves, enjoyed life, and suffered just as we do today. They lived according to a prescribed social pattern and they observed religious tenets as we do. Only through the work of the archaeologist, in company with the ethnologist and historian, can we weave together the threads in the fabric of Delaware's yesterday.

Bibliography

THE following is not a complete list of references consulted by the author, but is intended primarily as a compilation of source material relating to Delaware archaeology and to the ethnology of the tribes that once occupied the state. The additional titles relating to ossuaries and archaeology in neighboring states are set down as "bait" to lure the reader to delve deeper into the subject; neither is intended as a complete bibliography.

References from the *Bulletin* published by the Archaeological Society of Delaware are indicated *Bn.*

ARCHAEOLOGICAL EXCAVATIONS IN DELAWARE

(*In Chronological Sequence*)

Joseph Leidy, *Proceedings,* Academy of Natural Sciences, Phila., 1865, reporting meeting of June 20, 1865; *ibid.,* reporting meeting of October 23, 1866.

Francis Jordan, *Remains of an Aboriginal Encampment at Rehoboth, Delaware,* Speech made in 1880, published that year by the Numismatic and Antiquarian Society, Philadelphia, Pa.

———, Letter to Charles Rau, quoted in "Prehistoric Fishing in Europe and America," *Smithsonian Contribution to Knowledge,* Washington, D.C., 1884.

Hilborne T. Cresson, "River Dwellings in the Mud Flats of the Delaware River," *American Antiquarian,* Vol. 9, No. 6 (Nov. 1887), pp. 363–65.

———, "Early Man in the Delaware Valley," *Proceedings,* Boston Society of Natural History, Vol. 14, Part 2 (1888–89), pp. 141–50.

———, *Report Upon a Pile Structure in Naaman's Creek Near Claymont, Delaware,* Peabody Museum, Boston, 1892.

Francis Jordan, "Aboriginal Village Sites of New Jersey, Delaware and Maryland," *The Archaeologist,* Vol. 3, No. 4 (1895), pp. 99 ff.

Henry C. Mercer, *Researches Upon the Antiquity of Man in the Valley of the Delaware*, Publications of the University of Pennsylvania Series in Philology, Literature and Archaeology, Vol. 6, Philadelphia, 1897.

Francis Jordan, *Aboriginal Fishing Stations on the Coast of the Middle Atlantic States*, New Era Printing Company, Lancaster, 1906.

Joseph Wigglesworth, "Excavations at Rehoboth," *Bn.*, Vol. 1, No. 1 (May 1933), pp. 2–6.

D. S. Davidson, "Notes on Slaughter Creek," *Bn.*, Vol. 2, No. 2 (Oct. 1935), pp. 1–5.

——, "Burial Customs in the Delmarva Peninsula and the Question of Their Chronology," *American Antiquity*, Vol. 1, No. 2 (Oct. 1935), pp. 84–97.

H. Geiger Omwake, "Indian Burials in Delaware," *Bn.*, Vol. 3, No. 1 (May 1939), pp. 19–24.

C. A. Weslager, "An Aboriginal Shell Heap Near Lewes, Delaware," *Bn.*, Vol. 3, No. 2 (Oct. 1939), pp. 3–8.

A. Crozier, "Archaeological Notes on Claymont, Delaware, and Vicinity," *Bn.*, Vol. 3, No. 3 (Feb. 1940), pp. 3–6.

C. A. Weslager, "Shell Heaps of the Delmarva Peninsula," *Pennsylvania Archaeologist*, Vol. 11, No. 1 (Jan. 1941), pp. 17–23.

——, "Ossuaries on the Delmarva Peninsula," *American Antiquity*, Vol. 8, No. 2 (Oct. 1942), pp. 142–51.

—— and John Swientochowski, "Excavations at the Crane Hook Site, Wilmington, Delaware," *Bn.*, Vol. 3, No. 5 (May 1943), pp. 2–17.

ARTIFACTS FOUND IN DELAWARE

Harvard University, Twenty-second Report of Peabody Museum, Cambridge, Mass., Vol. 4, No. 2, 1888.

——, Twenty-third and Twenty-fourth Reports, Vol. 4, Nos. 3, 4, 1891.

W. K. Moorehead, *Stone Ornaments of the American Indian*, Andover, Mass., 1917.

W. Vernon Steen, "Historic Find at Dagsboro, Delaware" (Indian canoe), *Bn.*, Vol. 1, No. 2 (Jan. 1934), pp. 11–13.

William A. Cubbage, "Recent Find of Pottery in Kent County," *Bn.*, Vol. 1, No. 4 (May 1934), pp. 6–9.

John Noon, "Skeletal Remains from Slaughter Creek," *Bn.*, Vol. 2, No. 1 (March 1935), pp. 1–38.

D. S. Davidson, "Notes on Faunal Remains from Slaughter Creek," *Bn.*, Vol. 2, No. 4 (Oct. 1936), pp. 28–9.

Donald Horton, "Technological Study of Sherds from Slaughter Creek," *Bn.*, Vol. 2, No. 4 (Oct. 1936), pp. 29–34.

A. Crozier, "Delaware Folsom Points," *Bn.*, Vol. 3, No. 1 (May 1939), pp. 8–10.

C. A. Weslager, "Delaware Bannerstones," *Bn.*, Vol. 3, No. 1 (May 1939), pp. 11–17.

S. C. Robinson, "The Triangular Arrowpoint in Delaware," *Bn.*, Vol. 3, No. 3 (Feb. 1940), pp. 13–17.

Horace G. Richards, "Petrology of the Chipped Artifacts of the State of Delaware," *Bn.*, Vol. 3, No. 4 (Feb. 1941), pp. 5–9.

C. A. Weslager, "An Incised Fulgur Shell from Holly Oak, Delaware," *Bn.*, Vol. 3, No. 4 (Feb. 1941), pp. 10–15.

A. Crozier, "Birdstones," *Bn.*, Vol. 3, No. 4 (Feb. 1941), pp. 19–23.

Museum Inventories of Delaware Artifacts, Paper No. 4, Archaeological Society of Delaware, Wilmington, 1941.

Joseph Wigglesworth, *A Brief Archaeology of the Lenni Lenape,* privately printed, Wilmington, not dated.

C. A. Weslager, "Unexplored Sites in the Christina River Valley," *Bn.*, Vol. 3, No. 6 (Oct. 1938), pp. 8–10.

A. Crozier, "An Early Indian Village on the White Clay Creek, Delaware," *Bn.*, Vol. 3, No. 6 (Oct. 1938), pp. 4–7.

C. A. Weslager, *Coastal Aspect of the Woodland Pattern as Represented in Delaware,* Paper No. 1, Archaeological Society of Delaware, Wilmington, 1939.

William O. Cubbage, "Delaware Ceremonials," *Bn.*, Vol. 1, No. 4 (May 1934), pp. 7–9.

A. Crozier, "The Hog Swamp Site," *Bn.*, Vol. 4, No. 1 (May 1943), pp. 5–6.

SURVIVING NANTICOKE INDIANS

William H. Babcock, "The Nanticoke Indians of Indian River, Delaware," *American Anthropologist,* n.s. Vol. 1, No. 1 (Jan. 1899), pp. 273–82.

Royal B. Hassrick, "A Visit with the Nanticoke," *Bn.*, Vol. 4, No. 1 (May 1943), pp. 7–8.

Frank G. Speck, *The Nanticoke Community of Delaware,* Heye Foundation, Museum of the American Indian, New York, 1915.

Frank G. Speck, *Indians of the Eastern Shore of Maryland*, Eastern Shore Society, Baltimore, 1922.

———, *The Nanticoke and Conoy Indians*, Society of Colonial Dames, Wilmington, 1927.

———, "Back Again to Indian River, Its People and Their Games," *Bn.*, Vol. 3, No. 5 (May 1942), pp. 17–24.

———, "The Frolic Among the Nanticoke of Indian River Hundred, Delaware," *Bn.*, Vol. 4, No. 1 (May 1943), pp. 2–4.

C. A. Weslager, *Delaware's Forgotten Folk*, University of Pennsylvania Press, Philadelphia, 1943.

SURVIVING DELAWARE INDIANS

R. C. Adams, "Notes on the Delaware Indians," *Report on Indians Taxed and Not Taxed*, U.S. Census, 1890.

D. G. Brinton, *The Lenape and Their Legends*, Philadelphia, 1885.

M. R. Harrington, "Vestiges of Material Culture Among Canadian Delawares," *American Anthropologist*, n.s. Vol. 10, No. 3 (1908), pp. 408–18.

———, "Some Customs of the Delaware Indians," *Museum Journal*, Univ. of Penna., Vol. 1, No. 3 (1910), pp. 52–60.

———, "A Preliminary Sketch of Lenape Culture," *American Anthropologist*, n.s. Vol. 15, No. 2 (1913), pp. 208 ff.

———, *Religion and Ceremony of the Lenape*, Indian Notes and Monographs, Heye Foundation, Museum of the American Indian, New York, 1921.

———, *Dickon Among the Lenape Indians*, John C. Winston Co., Chicago, 1938.

Jasper Hill (Big White Owl), "My People the Delawares," *Bn.*, Vol. 4, No. 1 (May 1943), pp. 9–13.

Frank G. Speck, *A Study of the Delaware Big House Ceremony*, Penna. Historical Commission, Harrisburg, 1931.

———, *Oklahoma Delaware Ceremonies, Feasts and Dances*, American Philosophical Society, Philadelphia, 1937.

Gladys Tantaquidgeon, *A Study of Delaware Indian Medicine Practices and Folk Beliefs*, Penna. Historical Commission, Harrisburg, 1942.

OSSUARIES

Henry C. Mercer, "Explorations of an Indian Ossuary on the Choptank River, Dorchester County, Maryland," *Research upon the Antiquity of Man in the Valley of the Delaware*, Publications of the University of Pennsylvania in Philology Literature and Archaeology, Vol. 6, Philadelphia, 1897.

W. C. MacLeod, "Priests, Temples and the Practice of Mummification," *International Congress of Americanists*, 22nd Session, 1928, pp. 207–30.

T. D. Stewart and W. R. Wedel, "The Finding of Two Ossuaries on the Site of the Indian Village of Nacotchtanke" (Anacostia), *Journal of the Washington Academy of Sciences*, Vol. 27, No. 5 (May 1937), pp. 213–19.

T. D. Stewart, "The Finding of an Indian Ossuary on the York River in Virginia," *Journal of the Washington Academy of Sciences*, Vol. 30, No. 8 (August 1940), pp. 356–64.

Alice L. Ferguson, "An Ossuary near Piscataway Creek," *American Antiquity*, Vol. 6, No. 1 (July 1940), pp. 4–18.

T. D. Stewart, "An Ossuary on the Indian Village Site of Patawomeke," *Explorations and Field Work of the Smithsonian Institution*, Washington, 1940, pp. 67–70.

William J. Graham, *The Indians of Port Tobacco River, Maryland, and Their Burial Places*, privately printed, Washington, 1935.

ARCHAEOLOGY IN NEIGHBORING STATES

A few recommended titles relating to digging in the neighboring states of Pennsylvania, Maryland, New Jersey, and Virginia.

Mary Butler, *Three Archaeological Sites in Somerset County*, Pennsylvania Historical Commission, Harrisburg, 1941.

Donald Cadzow, *Archaeological Studies of the Susquehannock Indians*, Pennsylvania Historical Commission, Harrisburg, 1936.

———, *Petroglyphs in the Susquehanna River, near Safe Harbor, Pennsylvania*, Pennsylvania Historical Commission, Harrisburg, 1934.

Dorothy Cross, *The Archaeology of New Jersey*, Vol. 1, Trenton, 1941.

Gerard Fowke, *Archaeologic Investigations in James and Potomac Valleys*, Bureau of American Ethnology, Bulletin 23, Washington, 1894.

William H. Holmes, "Stone Implements of the Potomac-Chesapeake Tidewater Province," *Annual Report of the Bureau of American Ethnology*, XV, 13–157, Washington, 1897.

Carl Manson, Howard A. MacLeod, James B. Griffin, "The Culture of the Keyser Farm Site" (Virginia), *Papers of the Michigan Academy of Science, Arts and Letters*, XXIX (1944), 375–418.

Max Schrabisch, *Archaeology of the Delaware River Valley*, Pennsylvania Historical Commission, Harrisburg, 1930.

Richard E. Stearns, *The Hughes Site*, The Natural History Society of Maryland, Baltimore, Jan. 1940.

———, *Some Indian Village Sites of Tidewater Maryland*, The Natural History Society of Maryland, Baltimore, 1943.

Addendum

During the twenty-five years that have rolled by since I wrote *Delaware's Buried Past* many advances have been made in the field of archaeology, both in the Delaware River Valley and elsewhere in the United States. Information is now available which had not yet come to light in 1944, and obviously if I were writing the book today I would present the data in light of the latest available discoveries. For example, the doubt I expressed (page 157) about the validity of Indian place-names as applied to certain native villages in Delaware has been dispelled in a monograph which Dr. A. R. Dunlap and I have written. However, the personal anecdotes which I recounted, the historical notes about the work of the early archaeologists, the basic concepts of the origin of the Indians and their migrations, and the observations about geology are still as applicable as when they were written.

As I said in the Preface, the book was intended as a compilation of individual archaeological adventures in Delaware, and did not purport to offer any notable scientific contributions. This Addendum similarly does not contain an analysis of cultures or technical discussions, but is merely an extension of the original text to bring the reader up to date with some of the more important archaeological developments in the lower Delaware River Valley since 1944.

I refer to the lower Delaware Valley, instead of just the state of Delaware, because if anything has been learned from the archaeological investigations, it is that the cultures of the natives who lived on the fresh-water tributaries of the Delaware River in New Jersey in prehistoric times are closely related to those who lived in Delaware. The two sides of the river should be considered as one geographical region, a single, natural ecological zone which transcends state and county lines. The Delaware River is the central axis of the coastal plain areas of the two states, and the environmental conditions were the same on both sides of the river in precontact times. I said (page 143), "All things considered, New Jersey produces material closest in type to the artifacts found in Delaware." To some extent, but with certain less apparent similarities, the same thing might be said of the prehistoric cultures of the Eastern Shore of Maryland.

New Jersey's native population seems to have been larger than Delaware's, and the quantity of artifacts greater, as evidenced by the abundance of material uncovered on the forty New Jersey sites excavated by the Indian Site Survey under the direction of Dr. Dorothy Cross and on sites investigated by others. Yet, with the exception of "Iroquoian" pottery and smoking pipes, I believe it is accurate to say that practically all the common artifact types found in New Jersey, from bolos to bannerstones, can be found in Delaware collections. Artifacts from Delaware now even include a human effigy piece which was found under circumstances worth relating.

In the fall of 1955, the late Harold W. T. Purnell and others located and uncovered a burial pit at the Slaughter Creek Site containing human bones representing seventeen individuals. As in the characteristic multiple burials previously unearthed on the site, many of the bones were disarticulated and some of them were missing. The bones were removed and taken for identification and study to Dr. T. Dale Stewart at the U.S. National Museum in Washington, D.C., where it was learned, incidentally, that one of the remains was that of a male who stood six feet three inches—the tallest Indian reported from Delaware.

Dr. Stewart's laboratory assistant began to clean and repair the bones, some of which were still encased in blocks of sun-baked earth. Tasks like this are a real chore to the physical anthropologist, who prefers to examine a skeleton with all the bones intact, because the identification of age, sex, and physical type requires careful study of skull, teeth, and bones as an individual problem. As the assistant began wetting the hardened earth to separate the unrelated bones, she noted a small bone or antler fragment of unusual shape that had also been imbedded in the soil. Dr. Stewart immediately recognized it as a man-made carving, and thereafter each bit of earth was washed through a fine sieve and other little pieces of the artifact recovered and gradually fitted together.

When the pieces were finally assembled, the artifact, about five inches long, represented a row of five identical human figures, apparently standing erect, facing front, and connected to a base consisting of a horizontal piece of the same bone or antler, which was evidently intended to represent a canoe. There were two vertically drilled holes in the base, one on each side of the central figure. Although the original function of the artifact is unknown, a good guess is that it may have been an ornamental comb top, lashed by a thong strung through the two holes to a comb having wooden teeth, and perhaps worn to beautify the hair of an ancient Indian belle. The only other artifact found with the bones, in addition to fragments of shell-tempered pottery, was a polished awl made from a turkey bone. It was a paradox that the unusual carved bone or antler artifact, the first of its kind recorded for Delaware, was removed from Slaughter Creek soil by anthropologists hard at work miles away from the site!

Since 1944 there have been a number of significant developments in the organization for archaeological inquiry in both Delaware and New Jersey. The Archaeological Society of Delaware, formerly the only group in the state pursuing archaeological studies, in 1957 formed its first chapter, called the Minguannan Chapter for a historic Delaware Indian village on White Clay Creek; and in 1960 the Tancopanican Chapter was organized, perpetuating a traditional Indian name for the Brandywine.

Following the death in 1954 of Archibald Crozier, a long-time member and officer, the society established the Archibald

Crozier Memorial Award to be given "to a member of the Society for distinguished achievement in the advancement of archaeology during the current fiscal year." The first recipient of the Crozier Award in 1957 was Charles F. Kier, Jr., the society's president in 1956 and 1957.

After the death in 1963 of Mr. Crozier's widow, who had also been a member of the society over a long period of years, his books and Indian relic collection were subsequently sold to settle the estate. Fortunately, due to the efforts of some members of the society, approximately 2,000 artifacts which Mr. Crozier had collected during his lifetime of surface hunting on the Crane Hook and Stanton sites were acquired from the purchaser and are now part of the society's collection of some 20,000 artifacts.

There have been other deaths which have removed from the archaeological scene a number of individuals mentioned in the text, such as H. Geiger Omwake, Dr. J. Alden Mason, J. K. Spare, Dr. Frank G. Speck, Harold W. T. Purnell, and S. C. Robinson, who bequeathed his Indian collection to the Archaeological Society of Delaware in my care. This small but fine collection is now in storage with the society's other artifact holdings, awaiting the day when suitable facilities will be available for its display.

In Sussex County, Delaware, a new archaeological group was organized in 1948, first called the Sussex Archeological Association, later renamed the Sussex Society of Archeology and History.

In 1965 the Kent County Archaeological Association was formed, giving the state an investigatory group in each of its three counties.

On April 22, 1967 the Kent County Archaeological Association invited the other two groups to attend its annual meeting at Dover, and for the first time representatives of the three organizations were brought together in a joint meeting. It was my privilege to be invited as the guest speaker on this memorable occasion.

Of utmost significance, not only to the citizens of Delaware, but to the thousands of visitors from other states, was the opening, at long last, of a state museum at Dover on December 15, 1950, under the jurisdiction of the Public Archives Commission. This project was culminated through the tireless efforts of the state archivist, Dr. Leon de Valinger, Jr., a charter member and the first secretary-treasurer of the Archaeological Society of Delaware. The museum is housed in the old Dover Presbyterian Church, a fine old renovated building originally erected in 1790, thus preserving a structure in which Delaware's constitution of 1792 was drafted and ratified under the leadership of John Dickinson, penman of the Revolution. In 1951 an adjacent chapel building was modified and opened as a second building, and a third building was opened in 1955. The Indians of Delaware are represented in a permanent exhibit in a section of the museum devoted to archaeology, and special exhibits are arranged as needs require.

During the presidency of the late Dr. Walter Hullihen, the University of Delaware had cooperated with the Archaeological Society of Delaware by allocating a large basement room in the former Memorial Library at Newark, Delaware, for use as an archaeological workshop and museum, opened to the public on February 22, 1941 (page 69). Expanding enrollment and resultant shortage of space required the university to abandon the project in 1952. At the time the museum was opened there were no courses in anthropology offered at the university, and although the museum proved to be temporary, it provided impetus for an academic interest in archaeology.

Through the efforts of Professor Frederick Parker, chairman of the former Department of Sociology, the department was expanded into a broader Department of Sociology, Anthropology, and Geography, and courses in anthropology and archaeology are now part of the curriculum. This marked a significant milestone in advancing the study of archaeology in Delaware.

Of even greater significance was the creation of the State Archaeological Board by an Act of the General Assembly in 1953, a forward and progressive step which had many champions among the archaeological enthusiasts in Delaware. The objectives of the statute creating the board were to sponsor and encourage research in archaeology in Delaware, to protect prehistoric sites, to retrieve artifacts during the course of any public construction, to cooperate with educational institutions and archaeological groups in the state in preserving archaeological data and in instruction as to the manner of life of the early inhabitants; also to publish such material as it deemed pertinent.

Seven members of the board, according to the statute, were to be appointed by the governor from recommendations given him by seven specifically named organizations. The first members appointed by Governor J. Caleb Boggs were the following:

W. W. Mack, Chairman	State Highway Department
Kenneth Wilson, Secretary	State Museum
Dr. Frank Sommer	University of Delaware
Dr. C. A. Bonine	Sussex Society of Archaeology and History
H. Geiger Omwake	State Board of Education
Leon de Valinger, Jr.	State Archives
L. T. Alexander	Archaeological Society of Delaware

On January 30, 1965, the Archaeological Board employed Mr. Ronald A. Thomas as Delaware's first state archaeologist.

To cover in detail the work and findings of the three archaeological groups since *Delaware's Buried Past* was originally published would require a separate and much larger book as a sequel to this one, and I will leave that task for others. I will make only brief reference to certain of the major projects which I believe are the most important, and fuller detail may be found in the printed and mimeographed publications of the societies.

One of the most interesting projects conducted by the Sussex Society of Archeology and History was that within the town limits of Lewes—but it had nothing to do with Indians.

The purpose of the excavation was to locate the site of the fort built by the colonists sent by the Dutch patroons in 1631. The fort was subsequently destroyed by the Indians and the colonists massacred, and in time all traces of it apparently disappeared and there were many conflicting views about its original location. Archaeological investigation started in 1952 was continued in 1954, when postmolds of the palisade and north bastion were located. Ten years passed before permission could be obtained from the owners of the land to extend the digging, and in 1964, after permission was given, additional postmolds which originally belonged to the south bastion were uncovered. As a result of this work, Dr. C. A. Bonine, who was in charge, made drawings which show the exact location of the palisades and bastions of the fort, and the issue is no longer in doubt.

Work by members of the Sussex Society of Archeology and History at the Ritter Site, the Mispillion Site, and the Townsend Site, all in Sussex County, produced an abundance of artifactual, ceramic, and skeletal material. There have also been other investigations sponsored by this group, but the work at the Townsend Site near Lewes, which began in 1948, was outstanding in the data it produced. It permitted, from the 750 restorable pottery vessels which were uncovered, an identification of the typical late prehistoric pottery type (called Late Woodland), which was shell-tempered, fabric-impressed, conoidal in shape, having a slight constriction of the neck but a flush rim. The shape closely resembled the large vessel found at Slaughter Creek (illustrated opposite page 144). The Townsend excavation was more methodically conducted than the intermittent digging at Slaughter Creek, and very careful records were kept of artifact associations. The random digging by numerous individuals at Slaughter Creek did not permit keeping such records.

Skeletal remains of fifty-eight individuals were excavated at the Townsend Site, some were bundles of disarticulated bones, probably secondary burials, and others were found articulated and extended. These bones were subjected to very careful professional study, and the occupants were characterized as principally long-headed (dolichocephalic). The remains of twelve dogs confirmed our findings at Rehoboth in 1942 (page 86) that dogs were bred by the Indians of the bayshore.

The predominate triangular arrowheads, along with a pronounced bone, antler, and tortoise shell industry, provided traits for comparison in future excavations. Signs of fire in some of the shell pits at Townsend suggested to the excavators that the Indians may have cooked in them, which parallels observations we made at the Cedar Creek Site years before (pages 102–3). No white man's trade goods were found in association with Indian materials, which means that the Townsend people occupied their village before the Dutch settlement was made at nearby Lewes in 1631. However, all the archaeological evidence suggests that the village thrived just prior to the appearance of the white man in Delaware Bay; in other words, the site was not of any great antiquity, but it gives the archaeologist a good picture of the life of the coastal Indians when they were observed by the first white explorers.

In addition to the work at the Townsend Site, members of the Sussex Society made two interesting individual finds on southern Delaware sites worthy of mention. In 1955 H. Geiger Omwake and others found a cache of 179 argillite blades on a farm on the south side of Kiunk Ditch, a tributary of the St. Jones River. In 1951 James Parson uncovered a cache of 25 conch shells (*Busycon carica*) on the Derrickson farm near Lewes. The spiral ends of all the shells had been removed, which suggested that the shells were the raw material of beadmaking discarded by the Indian artisan. A bead of this type was found at the Mispillion Site.

Among the excavations conducted by members of the Archaeological Society of Delaware since 1944, of special interest was the project which established Indian occupancy at the rock shelter in Beaver Valley on a tributary of the Brandywine, the Ragan Tower Site near Newport, and the work at the Harlan Mill steatite quarry in Cecil County, Maryland. Excavations were also conducted on the documented Indian site called Minguannan on the west branch of White Clay Creek in London Britain Township, Chester County. On page 157, I pointed out that this site had not yet been excavated, but the excavation can now be counted among the developments since 1944. Members of the Minguannan Chapter worked on the northern and wooded end of this site for four years uncovering a considerable quantity of artifacts and restorable pottery. Material ranged from Archaic to Late Woodland, but no contact material was found at this particular section of the site.

Among the historical sites excavated by the society was a colonial log cabin on Old State Road near Wilmington in 1951–52. This cabin was subsequently moved to the State Museum, where it has been reconstructed as an exhibit with contemporary interior furnishing. On display are some of the coins, buttons, and white clay pipes from among the hundreds of objects recovered in the soil underneath the cabin and presented to the museum by the society.

The Caleb Pusey house on Chester Creek in Upland, Pennsylvania, a one and one-half story, four-room structure, which had been continuously occupied for 280 years, is another historic site where the society is conducting archaeological investigations. Many artifacts, such as coins, buttons, gun flints, and large quantities of pottery, glass, and objects of metal were excavated beneath the house prior to its restoration as a historic shrine. Other historic archaeology has included work at the Price's Corner log cabin, Collins-Johnson house, Buck Tavern, Brandywine Academy, and the Lea Derickson house.

The Kent County Archaeological Association, the most recent of the Delaware groups, excavated the Colbourne Site on the Murderkill River as a society project, but its members have been closely associated with the state archaeologist, and have assisted him in his excavations. Mr. Thomas has conducted excavations at twelve different sites, under the auspices of the State Archaeological Board. The two projects of most significance were those at Massey's Landing on Long Neck between Rehoboth and Indian River bays and at Island Field near

Bowers Beach. The former site, which is closely related culturally to the Townsend Site, gives the archaeologist a view of a neighboring coastal village which survived into the historic period. This is evidenced by the white clay smoking pipes and other trade goods found in association with shell-tempered pottery and artifacts in three different shell pits. These artifacts and pottery were identical with those excavated at the Townsend Site.

Island Field at Bowers Beach, in its second season of excavation as this was written, contained a large aboriginal cemetery which to date has produced seventy Indian burials, and it is almost certain that additional graves will be uncovered as the investigation continues. Flexed burials, supine and loosely flexed, and a bundle burial of disarticulate bones, were uncovered during the 1967 digging. Many artifacts have been recovered, some of which, like the perfect platform pipe found in one of the graves, seem to be related to the midwestern mound cultures.

This pipe was found near the body of a ten-year-old child, probably placed in the grave as an offering by a member of his family. Among the other unusual artifacts unearthed at the Island Field Site (which is situated on the 200-acre Webb farm) was a ceremonial dish carved from a human skull, two Delaware Bay conch shells carved into drinking cups, a harpoon made of deer antler, shark teeth, a piece of mica, and a pendant of Ohio banded slate. It also was evident that some of the Indian remains had been cremated before they were placed in the ground, which also suggests an exotic mortuary custom. The identity of the aboriginal people who buried their dead at this site still remains a mystery to be solved by further archaeological work.

The state archaeologist has also made a number of other investigations, and he has offered a solution to the unusual phenomenon at Port Penn, namely the so-called Indian Holes (pages 146–48). He visited the site and obtained the permission to excavate denied me some years ago, but examination of one of the holes left him as much perplexed as I had been.

Some time later a note in a publication relating to the geology of Delaware gave him a clue. It seems that a band of green sand or marl used for fertilizer stretched from Port Penn to Noxontown Pond. During the nineteenth century, test holes were dug at various locations to find the marl, and Ronald Thomas has suggested that the Indian Holes at Port Penn may be the result of that testing. At least, that's the best explanation that has been offered to date.

The frontispiece of this book is a map drawn in 1944 by the Wilmington artist-archaeologist, John Swientochowski, showing the known Indian sites in Delaware. In 1964 the Delaware Archaeological Board undertook a project in cooperation with the three archaeological groups to conduct a methodical, state-wide site survey. An archaeological site was defined as a location in which a concentration of artifacts had been recovered, and the procedure called for dividing each county into blocks bounded by lines of latitude and meridians of longitude or state and county borders. Each block was given a letter designation, and each site was identified by number and letter translated to an official map, now in Ronald Thomas' custody, on which there are recorded almost 400 archaeological sites in the state.

NEW JERSEY

"As yet there is no record in Delaware of petroglyphs, or pictographs, as they are also called, which are designs representing animals, birds, and other figures scratched on the surface of boulders or rock outcroppings." That statement (pages 144–45) still stands, but if I had said the same thing about New Jersey a correction would now be in order.

Until 1965, petroglyphs had never been recorded for New Jersey, but a severe drought that year caused the water level of the Delaware River to drop, exposing areas of the upper shoreline which had been covered with water as long as the oldest resident could remember. It was on such an exposed beach that New Jersey's first petroglyph came to light. It was discovered by Jon and Rudyard Jennings near their summer home along the river in Walpack Township, Sussex County, New Jersey, about two and one-half miles below Dingman's Ferry.

The feature was a flat sandstone rock, five feet across its longest axis, five feet wide, weighing about a half ton. The rock was larger but otherwise no different in appearance from many others like it along the stream, with one important exception: it was marked with twenty-one well-preserved and readily identifiable stylized figures of men or animals, and twelve engravings of nonidentifiable forms. Each of the designs had been pecked and rubbed into the hard parent rock, apparently with a hammerstone.

Herbert C. Kraft, director of the university museum at Seton Hill University in South Orange, was contacted; and after obtaining the permission of the owners of the property, he removed the artifact and, to preserve it and prevent its loss to science, placed it in the custody of the Seton Hill Museum. Since there were no associated artifacts, there is no clue as to the date when the natives pecked the series of figures on the stone. Nor, for that matter, has anyone been able to explain the meanings of the inscribed figures, some of which appear to be likenesses of men with uplifted arms, some with arms flexed down; lizardlike creatures; bird tracks; and dogs or other mammals. One thing seems certain—these inscriptions laboriously executed on the hard surface of the rock were not idle doodlings, but why they were made and what they mean is locked up in the bosom of a nameless aboriginal artist, possibly a prehistoric Delaware Indian, who went to his eternal rest centuries ago.

Like the archaeological groups in Delaware, the Archeological Society of New Jersey, which now has three chapters and more than four hundred members, is actively engaged in investigating the archaeology of the state. The society, organized November 12, 1931, was an outgrowth of an advisory committee on Indian research attached to the New Jersey State Museum at Trenton. The members of the society continue to work closely with the museum, which has been expanded in recent years and where a full-time assistant curator of archaeology is now a member of the staff.

Since 1959 New Jersey's major archaeological interest has been focused along the upper Delaware River in Warren and Sussex counties, where the projected Tocks Island Reservoir will flood thirty-seven miles of the Delaware River Valley. Every effort is being made to locate the aboriginal sites in this area, excavate and preserve artifacts, and gather all possible data before the former native camp and village sites are inundated. Through funds jointly provided by the National Park Service, the New Jersey State Museum, and the Archeological Society of New Jersey, more than forty sites have been located so far, and a number of them have been excavated.

Among the archaeologists in New Jersey who have conducted individual digs in the state, one of the most widely known was educator Dr. Charles A. Philhower, who died in 1962 at the age of eighty-four. Dr. Philhower realized the dream of every amateur archaeologist when he purchased as his estate in 1922 a forty-five-acre tract located along the upper Delaware River opposite Minisink Island. His property was the site of the extensive Munsee Indian town of Minisink, recorded in historic times, although the site was occupied for a long time before the arrival of Europeans. Dr. Philhower conducted excavations on his property every summer for many years, uncovering between 175 and 200 Indian graves, opening 200 pits; and in doing so he gathered a large collection of artifacts which he presented to Rutgers University. In 1947 portions of the same site were excavated by Dr. William A. Ritchie, aided by a grant from the Indiana Historical Society.

One of the most enthusiastic nonprofessionals in New Jersey who has held offices in the archaeological societies of New Jersey and Delaware is Charles F. Kier, Jr. Less fortunate than Dr. Philhower, who had a major site almost at his back door, Mr. Kier engaged in an excavation in New Jersey during a 36-month period starting in February, 1952, and his most difficult problem was in reaching the site he had found and selected to dig. He was assisted by another amateur, Fred Calverley, and they conducted the investigations as a labor of love over weekends, holidays, and during vacations.

The site which they named Raccoon Point was located in the tidal marshes of the Delaware River drainage system, southwest of Bridgeport in Gloucester County. Secluded, overgrown, and extremely difficult to reach because of a creek and the soggy marshes surrounding it, the former prehistoric Indian fishing village was accessible only on foot, and, at certain times, hip boots had to be worn. The two investigators were constantly beset with invasions of pesky New Jersey mosquitoes, and at the end of a hard siege of digging one spring day they found that the tide had moved in and inundated the marsh. Only through extreme difficulty were they able to get back to their car parked more than a mile away.

But in the long run the hardships they suffered paid off. With painstaking care, using approved archaeological methods, carefully measuring, taking notes, and photographing every stage of their work, they gradually amassed a large and interesting assortment of artifacts. When the project was completed the specimens numbered 1,798, representing thirty-three different kinds of tools and implements, ranging from arrowshaft smoothers, net sinkers, celts, grooved axes, and others, to 380 arrowpoints, 199 spearpoints, and 105 stone scraping tools. Potsherds numbered 4,820, including 477 fragments of steatite (soapstone) cooking vessels, which are believed to be older than clay pottery.

Entirely apart from the artifacts recovered, the data they developed contributed to the knowledge of Delaware Valley prehistoric cultures. Mr. Kier presented this information in a lengthy report which was published by the Society for Pennsylvania Archaeology, and he concluded that the Raccoon Point Site was occupied over a long period of time, first by archaic Indians (much earlier than the Townsend Site people), who had no pottery vessels and used very crude tools; later by a people who made and cooked in stone pots; and still later by Indians further advanced in their culture who had progressed to making flat-bottomed clay vessels. Finally the site was occupied by the later Woodland Indians, who made round- and pointed-bottomed clay vessels.

Mr. Kier found only fragments of the flat-bottomed pots, but they were doubtless similar in appearance to the vessel uprooted by a bulldozer in 1955 in a farm field at Turnip Patch Point on the north side of Pepper Creek, Sussex County, Delaware. Sufficient sherds were recovered there by Roger Vandergrift of Millville, Delaware, to permit restoration of three fourths of the grit-tempered, flat-bottomed vessel, whose extraordinary shape was compared to that of a small coal scuttle.

As the archaeologist reviews the discoveries made by Mr. Kier and others, he inclines to accept the theory that Delaware and New Jersey were first occupied by an archaic people who had not yet learned to make pottery; then flat-bottomed vessels cut from soapstone deposits came into existence; these were followed by flat-bottomed vessels of clay; and finally, and at the highest stage of Indian development, the round- and conoidal-bottomed pottery vessels, which were in use when the coastal Indians were first seen by white men. With this evolution in pottery styles there were also changes in other types of artifacts at different time periods.

COASTAL ADENA SITES

The most exciting discoveries recently made in the Delaware and Chesapeake bay areas are the implements and ornaments similar to those made by certain of the mound-building peoples of the Midwest. History has a strange way of repeating itself, and once more, as in the days of Atwater, Squier and Davis, Morgan, and Lapham (pages 16–20), the eyes of eastern archaeologists have been turned westward. To understand what has happened, let me set the stage for this exciting drama.

Shortly before and after the beginning of the Christian Era, there lived in the upper Ohio Valley a group of natives who built earthworks, lived in circular houses clustered together in fairly large communities, and in a late stage of their development practiced agriculture on a limited scale. They have been called the Adena people, a name derived from the name of an estate on the Scioto River near Chillicothe, given by its owner, Thomas Worthington, an early Ohio governor. In 1902 an archaeologist excavated a mound on the estate, and he called the cultural complex he found there the Adena.

The principal centers of the Adena people were on the Scioto River in Ohio and on the Kanawha River in West Virginia. They cremated many of their dead and buried the burnt bones in small rectangular log tombs which they covered with low earthen mounds. Successive additions of log tombs, each covered with new earth, increased the size of the mounds. Artifacts of rare form and apparently of considerable value to the natives were often buried with the cremated remains as grave offerings. Others of the select Adena dead were interred without cremation in an extended position, singly or in groups, but in larger tombs over which mounds were also built, and artifacts of fine workmanship were also buried with them. The Adena people also placed red ochre with their dead.

Since the majority of the Adena dead were cremated, the only skeletons available for study are those of the individuals, selected for unknown reasons, to be buried in the flesh. These people were round-headed (brachycephalic) and long-faced, and their heads were flattened in the back, a deformity caused by deliberately binding the head when the individual was in his infancy or strapping the child to a cradle board. To some anthropologists this flattening of the head suggests Central American influence, leading to a hypothesis that the Adena people originated in Mexico or elsewhere in Central America. Others disagree with this theory and believe the Adena culture was a natural outgrowth of archaic groups native to the Ohio Valley.

The Adena people used copper extensively for bracelets, pendants, beads, finger rings, small breastplates, and other artifacts. They buried these copper objects with their dead, along with mica, both in thick blocks and in sheets frequently cut in the shape of a crescent. Grave goods also included blocked-end tubular pipes of sandstone or fireclay; slate and sandstone gorgets of diverse shapes; unperforated stone tablets, some engraved with designs; large leaf-shaped blades and spearheads of flint; disc-shaped shell beads; hematite cones, et cetera. Although the Adena people made crude clay pottery vessels, very rarely are these containers ever found in their burial mounds.

The Adena, who are now believed to be the first builders of earthworks in the central and upper Ohio Valley, were followed in the Ohio Valley by another prehistoric mound culture of primarily long-headed (dolichocephalic) people called the Hopewell. They constructed earthworks in the form of circles, squares, rectangles and octagons, and were the makers of fine platform pipes. Hopewellian burial customs had strong similarities to Adena, but the Hopewell people received so much attention by the early investigators of the mound cultures that the separate identity of the earlier Adena was obscured for many years. The recognition in recent years of the Adena as a separate cultural manifestation was an outgrowth of the investigations of the Hopewell, and the recognition that the Adena were culturally older than the Hopewell has led to increasing archaeological attention being directed to the Adena.

For a time the occupations of the Adena and Hopewell overlapped, and some scientists hold to the opinion that Hopewell pressures resulted in a movement of late Adena people out of the Ohio Valley, and that some of them migrated to the east coast and the northeast. As evidence in support of this theory they point to the artifacts found on eastern sites which are strikingly similar to some of those uncovered in the Adena mounds.

The ornaments, spearheads, gorgets, and stone tubes found at a prehistoric burial ground on a high bluff at Sandy Point near Cambridge, Maryland (page 56), are believed by some scientists to have been carried east by Adena migrants. If so, this would suggest that the skeletal remains at Sandy Point, uncovered when the rare objects were found, estimated by one of the diggers to represent about one hundred people, may have been Adena wanderers, although this is by no means a certainty.

I first reported the Sandy Point discovery to the scientific world in a paper I wrote in October, 1942 for *American Antiquity* (page 166), although I was not present when the random digging occurred. At that time I knew next to nothing about the Adena, nor were other archaeologists in Maryland and Delaware aware of the similarities between Adena material and that found at Sandy Point. I visited three of the men who had collected specimens from the site, and I recognized that the objects were significantly different from artifacts found on local Maryland and Delaware sites. I said in my paper that these unusual artifacts were unquestionably exotic and that this influence was "probably from the southeast, bringing new burial customs and foreign material culture elements," but at that time no questions had yet been raised in the scientific literature about the possible eastward extension of the midwestern people themselves. That was to come later. With the limited published information then available I tentatively interpreted the complex as an association with burials of the great men of the eastern groups, a theory which has a basis in the seventeenth century historical literature of Virginia and Maryland.

Although there is now evidence which can be interpreted as lending weight to those who theorize that the Adena people migrated to the East, this view is by no means unanimously shared by anthropologists. Dr. James B. Griffin of the University of Michigan wrote in 1961 that he did not believe the evidence was sufficiently conclusive to support the thesis that the Adena people were driven from their homes by the intrusion of Hopewell people and fled to the east coast and northeast. He pointed out that the exotic burial goods, such as that found in Delaware, "may represent luxury items imported from the west and buried with the local dead."

When we objectively review the ever-increasing occurrences of this Adena-like material in Delaware, we are left with many unanswered questions. For example, the James L. Banning collection which I obtained some years ago for the Archaeological Society of Delaware, contains a stone tube, a gorget, and two large flint spearheads found together near the present Marine Terminal near Wilmington many years ago. The well-known Crane Hook Indian Site was located not far distant.

In 1933 along Brown's Branch, a tributary of the Murderkill, workmen digging a pit to obtain sand and gravel (the term borrow pit is locally used) uncovered human bones, stone tubes, and other Adena-like artifacts.

In 1938 a state highway crew, working in a similar borrow pit near Killens Mill Pond east of Felton, Delaware, in the Murderkill drainage system, uncovered a number of skeletons and associated artifacts. Among the artifacts were large blades and spearheads of Ohio flint, slate gorgets of various types, and a number of small lanceolate blades of white quartz. Mixed with the exotic material were arrowheads of local quartz, quartzite, and pebble jasper.

In 1954 the question of possible eastern extension of the Adena was first advanced by professional archaeologists as a result of excavations conducted by a Maryland amateur archaeologist, T. Latimer Ford, at the so-called West River Site situated on the edge of a fifty-foot cliff about one mile upstream from the west side of Chesapeake Bay. Approximately half the site had eroded away, but the remaining area, and the foot of the bluff where the eroded dirt had fallen, produced the same kind of spectacular artifacts recorded for Sandy Point. The site produced cremated human bones, unlike the bones found at Sandy Point, which were not cremated. Lumps of red ochre and charcoal were found associated with the remains.

The total number of artifacts recovered on the site, as well as those picked up at the base of the cliff, included 18 stone tubes, 33 blades and spearpoints, seven one-hole gorgets, 11 flat-based quartz spearpoints, three hematite cones, 26 miscellaneous small points, a piece of grooved hematite, four sharks teeth, two copper beads, and a siderite cone. The artifacts were made of Ohio fireclay, Ohio flint and banded slate,

Indiana limestone and flint, West Virginia flint, and jasper from the Indian quarries at Vera Cruz, Pennsylvania.

Mr. Ford showed me examples of these artifacts after the discovery was made, and although there could be no question of the Adena resemblance of the tubes, spearpoints, gorgets, and hematite objects, I was struck by the fact that the small points were very similar to those commonly found on local Maryland and Delaware sites.

In the summer of 1960 an accidental discovery led to the excavation of a site in Delaware producing Adena- and possibly Hopewell-related materials, which is probably the most important prehistoric site yet recorded for the state. It was accidentally discovered by a commercial contractor during the removal of gravel from the second terrace bordering the east side of St. Jones River not far distant from the Dover Air Force Base. During the gravel removal, bones and artifacts were exposed in the wall of the excavation, which prompted several boys to begin burrowing in the bank for Indian relics. The site was not a mound, but a sandy rise of a higher elevation than the land bordering the river. The terrace was adjacent to a series of sites along the St. Jones River well known to local surface collectors, and I had often walked through these fields where the late H. Geiger Omwake introduced me to Kent County archaeology thirty years ago. We often crammed our pockets with the usual type of artifacts found in Delaware fields — but we had never found anything to compare with the unusual discoveries made in 1960.

One of the boys brought some copper beads to the Delaware State Museum and showed them to Dr. Leon de Valinger, Jr., whose interest was promptly aroused, and after some persuasion he convinced the boy to show him where he had found the beads. When de Valinger visited the site, still under excavation by the contractor, he immediately recognized that the artifacts the boys were grubbing out of the sand were extremely unusual. He found the owner of the property and induced the man to call a halt to the operations, and de Valinger undertook a salvage project under the auspices of the state museum. He also brought the matter to the attention of the Archaeological Society of Delaware, and some of the members assisted in the work. De Valinger also sought technical advice from Dr. Don W. Dragoo of the Carnegie Museum in Pittsburgh, an authority on the Ohio Valley cultures, who visited the site while the work was in progress, as did Dr. J. Alden Mason and Dr. Jacob Gruber.

The bones of an estimated fifty-two individuals were found in a series of shallow, wide pits, and their disarticulated remains had been placed in the pits as bundles similar to burials uncovered at the Slaughter Creek and Townsend sites. The majority of the bones were *not* burnt, although a few were, and there were a few small heaps of burnt bones suggesting cremation. Red ochre was associated with some of the graves.

Approximately three hundred artifacts were found, but what was most unusual was that the majority of the exotic artifacts were contained in two large caches separate from the graves. These artifacts consisted of stemmed and leaf-shaped blades of Flint Ridge, Ohio, and Harrison County, Indiana, flint; a two-hole copper gorget; a rectangular copper strip; a slate gorget known as an expanded center bar; four rectangular gorgets with slightly concave sides; a trapezoidal two-hole gorget or pendant; three block-end tubes; a quantity of rolled copper beads; and Marginella shell beads. Pictures of the two caches *in situ* showed me by Dr. de Valinger indicate the spearpoints, blades, and gorgets of varying shapes were all placed together in a horizontal layer, although not in any orderly fashion. Dr. de Valinger also told me that, at a level *lower* than the caches of the exotic material, points of local quartz and quartzite were found *in situ*.

It was Dr. Dragoo's judgment that the material seemed to represent a very late Adena complex that had been influenced by Hopewell. It was also his opinion that this site, as well as the two Maryland sites, confirmed a hypothesis previously advanced by Dr. William A. Ritchie and himself, namely, that the material represented the artifacts of the migrant Adena people forced to leave the Ohio Valley with their prized possessions because of Hopewell pressure.

If this hypothesis is correct, then an extraordinary number of Adena people must have migrated to Delaware and Maryland, for in the spring of 1964 another parallel incident occurred near Frederica, Delaware, in the Murderkill drainage system (a few miles south of the St. Jones site). An independent contractor was digging sand and gravel from a borrow pit on the Isaacs farm to supply the State Highway Department in a road-building project. When the loads of sand and gravel were delivered, the workmen began to find unusual Indian artifacts, and the inspector traced the origin back to the borrow pit. Before long a number of workmen were digging and scraping in the banks of the pit and taking home quantities of artifacts. The scavenging evidently occurred over a period of weeks without any local archaeologists knowing about the discovery, and very large quantities of artifacts were removed from the borrow pit as the commercial digging progressed.

As in the instance of the St. Jones discovery, the news of what was happening eventually reached Dr. de Valinger at Dover, who immediately hurried to the site, located the owner, and tried to have the pothunting stopped. But it was too late; the newspapers had gotten wind of the story, and when the accounts appeared, curiosity seekers came from far and wide. Members of the state's archaeological groups attempted salvage operations over the Memorial Day weekend of 1964, but it was impossible to control the number of outsiders, who brought almost every kind of digging tools from garden spades to clam rakes.

No one knows how many artifacts had been previously removed by the workmen and curiosity seekers — nor how many were found over the Memorial Day weekend. Efforts were later made by members of the State Archaeological Board, with some success, to convince those who had found artifacts to bring them to be photographed. As a result of this foresight, photographs of some of the material are available (see oppo-

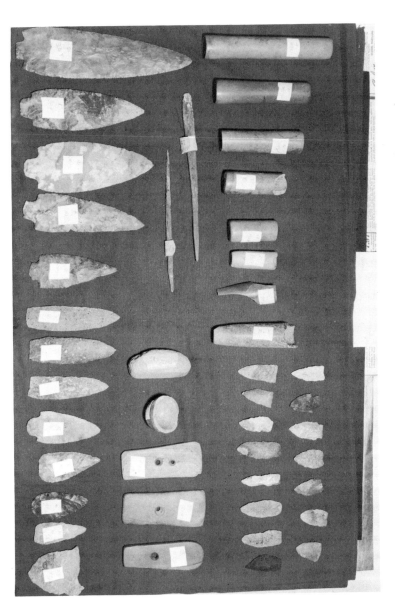

Representative artifacts from Isaacs Farm on the Murderkill Creek near Frederica, Delaware. Tubes at upper left and large flint spearpoints below are typical of the Adena material found here and on the St. Jones Site, although smaller points resemble local artifacts. (Courtesy of Delaware State Archives)

site) and a few representative pieces were later acquired by the state museum, where they are on display.

This site, like the one at St. Jones, was on a sandy rise, and it was also a burial place as indicated by the quantities of human bones that were removed. The burial site was also adjacent to a well-known coastal Woodland site, and it was uncertain whether the local arrowheads, which diggers found with the exotic materials, were all in the same levels. The experienced archaeologists uncovered over six hundred copper beads which the pothunters had overlooked, and salvaged a copper breast-plate; but regrettably almost all the spectacular blades, spear-points, tubes, hematite cones, paint cups, gorgets, and pendants were retrieved by persons who scraped, grubbed, shoveled, and raked, indifferent to anything except the notion of enriching themselves with Indian relics.

As a result of what turned out to be an uncontrolled and dis-organized treasure hunt, rare information relating to the Adena issue and which might have given answers to the questions which still remain unanswered was destroyed. Until a thorough study is made of some future site, which yet remains to be found, the mystery remains unsolved. Did the Adena people actually migrate and settle in Delaware? If so, were they ab-sorbed by the local Woodland Indians? If not, what happened to them? Did they then move up the Delaware River as has been suggested? If so, they could not have had many Ohio artifacts left in their possession when one considers the quanti-ties left in Delaware. Or was the migration strictly a myth, and were the Adena and Hopewell materials imported from Ohio by the local Delaware prehistoric groups and used by them as grave accompaniments?

Some benefits usually result from misfortune, and that is ex-actly what transpired following the looting of the Frederica Site. Incensed over what occurred, members of the State Archaeological Board made a strong representation to the Delaware General Assembly, citing the irreparable loss to sci-ence of invaluable data, and recommending the employment of a state archaeologist who would thereafter maintain a close rapport with contractors and highway officials, and would also organize a well-planned program to study Delaware archaeology. That is what happened, and that is how Delaware's first state archaelogist received his appointment.

PALEO-INDIANS

One of the first questions asked an archaelogist after he has excavated an aboriginal site, or when an unusual artifact is brought to him for identification, is, "How old is it?" Unfortunately, a reply in general terms seldom satisfies the questioner, and the archaeologist is invariably pressed to name a specific date. The development of the radiocarbon (Carbon 14) dating method, is a very useful tool in arriving at dates, but it can be used only with certain organic materials, not stone; and within the system there can be discrepancies. The organic matter must be uncontaminated; and in order to date stone artifacts, the organic material must be found in association, and a time period established for the organic matter, such as wood, charcoal, bone, and fabric, for example, before a date can be safely applied to the associated stone objects.

In Delaware and New Jersey certain speculations have been made as to the age of stone artifacts based on dates established in other states by means of radiocarbon techniques. Although certain inferences may be drawn, it is premature to name specific dates for prehistoric artifacts found in the Delaware-New Jersey areas other than on a very tentative basis. An exact chronology that will permit calendrical dating of various kinds and shapes of stone artifacts still remains to be developed for the Delaware Valley. In view of the lack of radiocarbon dates for a sufficient representative number of local sites, the safe and conservative approach is to speak in general terms, without naming dates. The amateur would do well to heed this caution, and the professional archaeologist will be relieved not to be pressed for opinions that cannot be scientifically supported.

Broadly speaking, the term Woodland Stage can be assigned

to the prehistoric Indian cultures which were at a high stage of development when the first Dutch explorers like Hendricksen and Mey first entered Delaware Bay in the early seventeenth century. Earlier periods of the Woodland Stage extended farther back into prehistoric times with different types of artifacts probably characterizing the different periods, but this information is still inexact. Earlier than the Woodland Stage, there was an Archaic Stage, in which the first clay pottery appeared and in which the artifacts differed from those found in the Woodland Stage. In other states where dating systems have been refined, archaeologists have a basis for referring to Late and Early periods of this Archaic Stage, but in the Delaware Valley these periods have not yet been clearly resolved in terms of time spans.

An even older chapter of man's existence on the North American continent is called the Early Hunter Stage. During this primitive stage the people which Dr. Frank H. H. Roberts, Jr., termed Paleo-Indians — ancestors of the later Indians — pursued mammoth, mastodon, ground sloth, a defunct species of bison, and other prehistoric animals now extinct. These Paleo-Indians had not yet developed pottery nor the bow and arrow, and had no knowledge of agriculture. They were nomadic huntsmen, and in the process of killing, cutting up, and devouring the flesh of the prehistoric mammals they used stone-tipped javelins and scrapers and knives having specialized flaking.

The existence of these Paleo-Indians in the Far West was proved by the recovery of the distinctly fluted Folsom points at Folsom, New Mexico; Lindenmeier, Colorado; Lubbock, Texas; the Brewster Site in eastern Wyoming, and elsewhere. The Folsom point has now been conclusively associated with animals of the Late Pleistocene, particularly the remains of extinct bison.

I said on page 152 that "Future research may, of course, reveal the existence in America of a people who were here prior to the coming of Folsom man." This has proved to be a correct assumption, for another more generalized type of

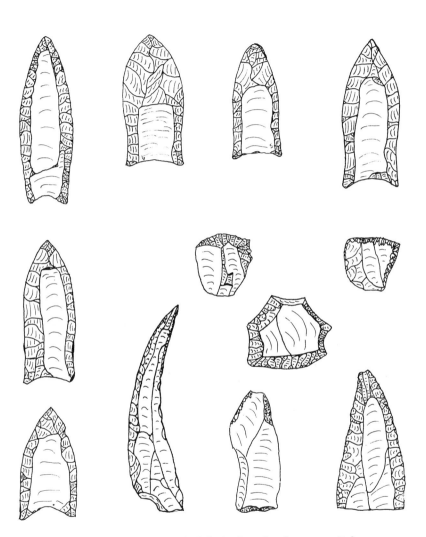

Typical fluted points and unifacially-flaked side and end scrapers, Delaware surface finds, probably handiwork of Paleo-Indian hunters. Drawings by Joseph S.
Hughes, courtesy of Delaware Archaeological Board.

fluted point, termed the Clovis, has since been found, and the evidence is clear that it was made by earlier hunters than those who made the Folsom points.

Excavations beginning in 1934 at Blackwater Draw near Clovis, New Mexico, by John L. Cotter of the Philadelphia Academy of Natural Sciences revealed an upper strata containing Folsom points in association with extinct bison, and below this layer were the remains of two mammoths having in association four points of the style since known as Clovis points. These points were similar to three points found in 1932 by scientists of the Denver Museum of Natural History at Dent, Colorado, in association with a large concentration of mammoth bones.

Since the discovery at Blackwater Draw, Clovis points have been found in association with mammoth remains at Domebo Canyon, Oklahoma; Lehner Ranch Arroyo, New Mexico; Miami in the Texas Panhandle; Naco, Arizona; and elsewhere.

Archaeologists have concluded from these discoveries that there were two separate groups of primitive hunters: the earliest, primarily mammoth killers, who made Clovis points, followed by a group who were primarily bison killers who made Folsom points. Carbon dating of the mammoth bones found in association with the Clovis points has dated the Clovis people to 9000 B.C. It is believed that they arrived in America from Asia about 12,000 or 13,000 years ago and moved down an ice-free corridor through Alaska and western Canada into the unglaciated parts of what is now the United States.

The true Folsom point can be readily distinguished from the Clovis point by the nature of the fluting, which is really the scar left on the stone when the flake was struck off. The fluting of a Folsom point consists of a single channel on each surface that extends all the way to the tip of the point, or nearly so; and the edges are delicately chipped. In other words, the maker struck off one large flake on either side of the point, evidently to make it easier to fit the end of a wooden shaft. A Clovis point is typically larger, with more coarsely chipped edges; and more than one flake was removed from each surface to produce the flute channels. These are normally broken out less than half way to the tip in what is called a hinge fracture. I pointed out (page 152) that the fluted points found on the surface in the East, which were then termed Folsom points, were "not true Folsom points, but may be classed as Folsom-like, and present a problem of great interest." It is now clear that what were called Folsom points in Delaware twenty-five years ago were more like the Clovis points which have since been found in the West.

Twenty-five years ago there was considerable doubt whether the Paleo-Indians actually made their way to eastern America, but the increasing number of fluted points found in the East now leads archaeologists to believe that the javelin-wielding, prepottery hunters reached the Atlantic seaboard as they pursued the herds of game now extinct. What happened was that during the period of the last glaciation the ice sheet that advanced down the North American continent forced the northern animals southward in search of sufficient vegetation to feed on. As these animals moved into the Delaware Valley it is likely that they were followed by bands of Paleo-Indian hunters. There is ample evidence that the mastodon and mammoth lived along the Atlantic seaboard during the Pleistocene or Ice Age, although no fluted points, or other evidences of man, have yet been found in the East with their fossilized remains.

To date no remains of these huge mammals have yet been uncovered in Delaware, but that does not necessarily mean they were not here, because the bones of the mastodon have been found as close as Mannington Township in Salem County, New Jersey, and at Reading in Berks County, Pennsylvania. Mammoth remains were found as close as Chadds Ford in Chester County, Pennsylvania. No artifacts were associated with any of these discoveries.

The mastodon remains in Mannington Township found in August, 1869, in a marl pit at Swedes Bridge on the farm of Joseph Hackett excited wide attention. The head was described in newspaper accounts as being five feet long, weighing

400 pounds; the under jaw weighed 120 pounds, and a rib bone measured four feet in length. The bones were removed and exhibited at an agricultural fair at Salem and then transferred to Rutgers University, where they are now on display in the museum of Geology Hall.

A number of surface sites where Paleo-Indians apparently camped and chipped out their distinctive fluted points and stone knives and scrapers have now been recorded in the East. One of these sites near the town of Enterline in central Pennsylvania produced sixteen whole or virtually intact fluted points, twenty-six broken points, including half of the base of each, and a large quantity of scrapers. These artifacts were all made of a distinctive flinty stone found in New York state which has been termed Onondaga chert and which suggests the Paleo-Indian hunters may have entered Pennsylvania from the north. In Dinwiddie County, Virginia, a workshop site of the makers of fluted points was found where fifty-eight points and fifty side scrapers were recovered. At Bull Brook near Ipswich, Massachusetts, several hundred specimens were found, and other eastern sites have produced fluted points.

The number of fluted points recorded for the Delaware River watershed is now in excess of one hundred. New Jersey has produced more than fifty-five, including four broken pieces from the Abbott farm, and Delaware can now account for at least thirty. In 1944 there was record of only ten for Delaware. These points are related by type, although not material, principally to Clovis, and some are similar to Enterline types. In addition to the fluted points, there have also been found on surface sites in Delaware a number of specimens of the typical Paleo-Indian flaked end scraper and elongated side scraper. Since these are difficult to describe, the accompanying ink sketches will acquaint the reader with their appearance. The Paleo-Indian scrapers are typically flaked on one side of the specimen only, which has resulted in their being described as "unifacially flaked."

Although indications in the East of the transient stay of the Paleo-Indians are still confined to scattered fluted points and

scrapers and to surface sites where these objects were apparently made, the archaeologist lives in constant hope of
finding a kill site where the fluted points, scrapers, and the
bones of the slain animals will all be uncovered in one complex
as in the West. When that happens, it will be archaeology's
most thrilling moment, because it will prove the hypothesis
that the Paleo-Indian hunters pursued and killed prehistoric
mammals, which have been extinct in the East for several
thousand years. The age-old question of the antiquity of Man
in eastern America will then have a definitive answer.

Additional References

The *Bibliography* on pp. 165–70 is still recommended as a starting point for the reader interested in Delaware archaeology; those interested in New Jersey will note the inclusion of Dorothy Cross, *The Archaeology of New Jersey* (Vol. 1, 1941), to which can now be added *The Abbott Farm* (Vol. 2, 1956), by the same author.

The following additional references cover data included in the Addendum, and are recommended for the reader who desires to delve deeper into the separate topics.

PLACE-NAMES

A. R. Dunlap and C. A. Weslager, *Indian Place-Names in Delaware*, Archaeological Society of Delaware, 1950.

UNUSUAL ARTIFACTS

T. D. Stewart, *A Unique Carved Bone Object from Delaware*, Delaware State Museum *Bulletin* No. 1, Dover, 1958 (illustration of comb top on p. 9).

H. G. Omwake, "A Unique Flat-Bottom Pottery Vessel from Delaware," *Bulletin*, Archeological Society of New Jersey, No. 11 (May 1956), pp. 1–2 (illustration of vessel).

Herbert C. Kraft, "The First Petroglyph Found in New Jersey," *Pennsylvania Archaeologist*, Vol. 35, No. 2 (August 1965), pp. 93–100 (illustration of petroglyphs).

EXCAVATIONS MENTIONED IN ADDENDUM

C. A. Bonine, "The South Bastion of DeVries Palisade," *The Archeolog*, (Publication of the Sussex Society of Archeology and History), Vol. 15, No. 2 (1964), pp. 13–19.

H. G. Omwake, *The Mispillion Site, Bulletin* (Archaeological Society of Delaware), n.s., No. 1, 1962.

The Townsend Site Near Lewes, Delaware, ed. by H. G. Omwake and T. D. Stewart, *The Archeolog*, Vol. 15, No. 1 (1963).

Seal T. Brooks, "The Beaver Valley Rock Shelter Near Wilmington, Delaware," *Bulletin* (Archaeological Society of Delaware), Vol. 4, No. 5 (January 1949), pp. 22–27.

C. A. Weslager, "Excavations at a Colonial Log Cabin Near Wilmington, Delaware," *Bulletin, ibid.*, Vol. 6, No. 1 (April 1954), pages unnumbered.

William A. Ritchie, *The Bell-Philhower Site Sussex County New Jersey*, Prehistory Research Series, Indiana Historical Society, Vol. 3, No. 2 (October 1949).

Charles F. Kier, Jr., and Fred Calverley, *The Raccoon Point Site, An Early Hunting and Fishing Station in the Lower Delaware Valley, Pennsylvania Archaeologist*, Vol. 27, No. 2 (August 1957).

ADENA CULTURE

William S. Webb and Charles E. Snow, *The Adena People*, Reports in Anthropology and Archaeology, No. 6, University of Kentucky, Lexington, 1945.

William S. Webb and Raymond S. Baby, *The Adena People – No. 2*, Ohio Historical Society, 1957.

T. Latimer Ford, "Adena Traits in Maryland," *Bulletin 17*, Eastern States Archeological Federation, 1958, p. 10 (very brief abstract).

T. Latimer Ford, "Adena Sites in Maryland," *Miscellaneous Papers*, Archaeological Society of Maryland, No. 1 (July 1959), pp. 12–13.

Meril L. Dunn, Jr., "A General Survey of the Adena Culture on the Delmarva Peninsula," *The Archeolog*, Vol. 18, No. 2, 1966, pp. 1–10.

Don W. Dragoo, *Mounds for the Dead: An Analysis of the Adena Culture*, Annals of Carnegie Museum, Vol. 37, 1963.

William A. Ritchie and Don W. Dragoo, *The Eastern Dispersal of Adena,* New York State Museum and Science Service Bulletin, No. 379, Albany, 1960.

James B. Griffin, Review of *ibid., American Antiquity,* Vol. 26, No. 4 (April 1961), pp. 572–73).

PALEO-INDIAN IN THE EAST

John Witthoft, "A Paleo-Indian Site in Eastern Pennsylvania, An Early Hunting Culture," *Proceedings* (American Philosophical Society) Vol. 96, No. 4 (August 1952), pp. 464–95.

Ronald J. Mason, "Time-Depth and Early Man in the Delaware Valley," *Bulletin,* Archaeological Society of Delaware, Vol. 9, No. 1 (March 1958), pp. 1–10.

Ronald J. Mason, "Indications of Paleo-Indian Occupation in the Delaware Valley," *Pennsylvania Archaeologist,* Vol. 29, No. 1 (April 1959), pp. 1–17.

Ronald A. Thomas, "Paleo-Indian in Delaware," *Bulletin,* Delaware Archaeological Board, Vol. 2, No. 3 (Fall 1966), pp. 1–11.

Index

207